STUDENT UNIT GUIDE

A2 English Language
UNIT 5

Specification B

Module 5: Editorial Writing

Jo Barrett

Philip Allan Updates
Market Place
Deddington
Oxfordshire
OX15 0SE

Orders

Bookpoint Ltd, 130 Milton Park, Abingdon, Oxfordshire, OX14 4SB
tel: 01235 827720
fax: 01235 400454
e-mail: uk.orders@bookpoint.co.uk
Lines are open 9.00 a.m.–5.00 p.m., Monday to Saturday, with a 24-hour message
answering service. You can also order through the Philip Allan Updates website:
www.philipallan.co.uk

© Philip Allan Updates 2006

ISBN-13: 978-0-86003-919-8
ISBN-10: 0-86003-919-6

This guide has been written specifically to support students preparing for the
AQA Specification B English Language Unit 5 examination. The content
has been neither approved nor endorsed by AQA and remains the sole
responsibility of the authors.

Printed by MPG Books, Bodmin

Philip Allan Updates' policy is to use papers that are natural, renewable
and recyclable products and made from wood grown in sustainable forests.
The logging and manufacturing processes are expected to conform to the
environmental regulations of the country of origin.

P00790

A2 English Language

Contents

Introduction

■ ■ ■

Content Guidance

■ ■ ■

Questions and Answers

Introduction

About this guide

The aim of this guide is to help you prepare for **Unit 5: Editorial Writing**. It is intended as a revision aid, not a textbook. There are three sections to this guide:

- **Introduction** — this outlines the Unit 5 specification and explains the exam format. It identifies the areas you will be assessed on and the assessment objectives for this module.
- **Content Guidance** — this provides a guide to the skills, practices and ideas you need to be successful in Module 5, such as how to prepare the pre-release materials and write the commentary. It offers advice on how to write in various styles and formats.
- **Questions and Answers** — this includes sample questions from past papers, as well as A- and C-grade candidate answers and commentaries from the examiner highlighting the strengths and weaknesses of each answer.

How to use this guide

This guide will not replace the practice and hard work that you will need to do to develop the flexibility of your writing skills. Just buying it does not guarantee a high grade, nor does recording it onto tape and playing it while you sleep. Even leaving it under your pillow won't work — you will actually have to read it.

As a revision guide this book will show you how to make the best use of your time when revising and practising your reading and writing skills. What *you* must do is get hold of the pre-release materials and tasks from recent Unit 5 exams (you can order these from the AQA website, **www.aqa.org.uk**). You must study, analyse and imitate a wide range of styles. In many ways this is a direct continuation and progression from the work you did for your Unit 3 course-work; in fact, you might have already studied some of the genres in your AS year. Finally, you must practise writing the short commentaries. These resemble trimmed-down versions of the commentaries you did for your original writing pieces in Unit 3.

Studying English Language

A-level English Language is an approach to language study that always starts with texts from everyday life, including varieties of speech, writing, books, magazines, mobile phone conversations, radio scripts and internet chat. The key idea to bear in mind is that language varies because people and situations vary. Users have a range of repertoires of different kinds of language they can choose between. Different situations, including different purposes and audiences, make different demands on the genre (type of writing), register (style of writing) and tone (the sense of reader–writer relationship).

Module 5

Like Module 3, Module 5 is a writing production module designed to give you opportunities for studying, practising and reflecting on writing in different styles. In Module 3 you will have had an open choice about the topics and purposes of your writing, and several months in which to redraft.

Module 5 builds on the skills you used for Module 3 and gives you scope for creative expression within a more structured framework. You are given a set of source materials to prepare, and a specified audience and purpose for which to write. You have 1 week to prepare the materials and 2 hours and 30 minutes in which to write your draft. Module 5 is worth 15% of the whole A-level.

Skills and practices

The Unit 5 exam will test you on the following skills and practices.

(1) Reading and preparing materials
- close reading and understanding of the source materials
- summarising
- identifying fact and opinion
- organising and cross-referencing the texts
- understanding genre and context
- glossing unfamiliar words
- identifying conflicts in sources
- making effective annotations

(2) Planning and writing skills
- selecting the best question for your abilities
- Selecting an appropriate range of materials
- considering the stylistic features of the genre
- considering the audience and the purpose
- developing a consistent tone and register to suit the audience and the task
- establishing a cohesive discourse structure
- adapting complex materials for the task
- maintaining appropriate grammatical accuracy

(3) Commentary-writing skills
- evaluating and exploring the concepts and issues of your own writing
- conscious recognition of the process and structure of your writing

Assessment objectives

Your answers are marked according to assessment objectives (AOs). These are the criteria examiners use to identify and measure the different skills you have shown. The assessment objectives for Module 5, and their weightings as percentages, are as follows:

AO1 (5%)	Communicate clearly the knowledge, understanding and insight appropriate to the study of language, using appropriate terminology and accurate and coherent written expression.
AO2 (7.5%)	Demonstrate expertise and accuracy in writing for a variety of specific purposes and audiences, drawing on knowledge of linguistic features to explain and comment on choices made.
AO4 (2.5%)	Understand, discuss and explore concepts and issues relating to language in use.

What do the AOs mean?

Put simply, the AOs mean that you are assessed for your ability to express yourself clearly using the conventions of standard English, your ability to a write in an appropriate style for your audience and your understanding of ideas relating to how texts are structured and styled.

The most heavily weighted assessment objective is AO2. This assesses how well you have written for the given audience and kept to the demands of the task. You must read carefully the instructions in the question paper so that you focus your writing in the right way. Ask yourself:

- Who is my audience?
- Why am I writing?
- What tone and style are needed for this text to work?

Remember the four purposes of your original writing work: inform, instruct, entertain, persuade. Remember too that writing is often complex and many texts may have more than one purpose.

Assessment objective 4 relates directly to the commentary. How conscious are you of the processes involved in your writing? How much of the success in your writing was due to luck or intuition? Can you explain what you did?

Assessment objective 2 judges how well your writing fits the conventions of the genre and the needs of the audience. Identifying and maintaining an appropriate tone of voice are critical to success.

Choosing the question that is right for you is also important. You will have strengths and weaknesses in writing in different styles, and it is worth playing to your strengths.

introduction

The examination

One week before the examination you will receive, or collect, from your school or college two sets of pre-release material. These will be from 20 to 30 pages in length, depending on the amount of visual material involved.

Each pack will cover a different subject. This can be anything from 'Brass bands' to 'Gateshead Quays', 'Castles', 'Codes and ciphers', 'Rally driving', 'Potholing', 'Penguins', 'Van Gogh' or 'The history of the Wild West' — in short, almost any subject. What they will have in common is that they are made up of between 12 and 20 different texts (labelled A, B, C etc.). These texts will all be from different sources and have different purposes, audiences, contexts and, sometimes, bias.

In the week between receiving the materials and the examination you will need to get to know these texts better than you know your own family. In the exam you will be given the choice of four different tasks (two tasks for each set of materials). **You need to answer on just one task based on one set of materials.** You will have 2 hours and 30 minutes to plan and write this task and a short commentary. Note the following points:

- The tasks are always about 1,000 words long. You must produce a new document that draws on the source material (and nothing else) and unifies it into a new whole. The tasks may require you to write in a particular medium, genre, style or mode.
- In the commentary you should explain some of the significant decisions and choices you made when you wrote your text. You have about 150–200 words to do this.
- Your answer will be marked out of 70 — 60 marks for the task and 10 marks for the commentary.

Frequently asked questions and concerns

Q Will I annotate the packs correctly and in enough depth for the exam? How do I know what is relevant?

A You won't know exactly what is relevant until the exam, but you can still pick out the main ideas, the examples and the link passages.

Q I'm worried that I won't be able to put the text into my own words.

A You are allowed to use text straight from the sources *if it is suitable*, but it is usually more advisable to rewrite the material to suit the new context. Use a dictionary and thesaurus when you prepare to jot down simpler meanings if there's a problem.

Q I'm worried about doing enough preparation on the packs before the exam.

A You will have at least 7 days between receiving the packs and the exam. You need to be disciplined without stressing yourself.

Q Where do I pick up my packs of source material?

A Ask your exams officer or your teacher, who will tell you where and when.

Q Will I just waste time trying to find the information?

A Not if you have indexed and highlighted the material in an organised way.

Q I'm worried about completing the exam on time. It's a lot of words.

A 1,200 words in 150 minutes is not as bad as you think. Good preparation will buy you time as you won't waste any. Dividing your task into chunks is a good idea.

Q Ideas are sometimes repeated in different sources, and may even be factually different. What do I do then?

A The answer lies in the provenance of the source. When was it written? What sort of text mentions it? Discuss your final decision in the commentary to justify your choice.

Q Some sources are lexically complex and have difficult lexical fields in them. What can I do about words I don't understand?

A Use a dictionary or thesaurus and write an easier word in the margin. You could talk about the materials with someone who does understand them (not your teacher, obviously).

Q If it's a topic I'm not interested in, I won't be able to write about it very well.

A You have to challenge yourself to be professional. Commissioned writers won't always like the subjects they are given. You have to work on your enthusiasm, or at least your understanding, to cope with the job.

Content Guidance

This section introduces editorial writing skills and processes. Being able to write in a range of genres, following a brief and maintaining an appropriate tone are critical to success. It is not a matter of learning facts and figures, but of understanding and accomplishment, which come from practice and reflection.

Editorial writing

Being a writer

Editorial writing is not an obscure or exotic skill. We all do it as we pass through the education system and go on to do it in many types of job. Any kind of preparation of materials for a reading public will involve editorial writing. We are all writers in one way or another, and will become more so with greater demand for literacy in our society and as the possibilities of the internet open up publishing.

Common skills and practices

It is worth looking at a few examples of the tasks previously set in the Unit 5 exam in order to clarify the skills and practices being tested. A list of these is given on pp. 74–76.

What these tasks have in common is their range of potential source materials and the practices you should exercise when you write. So, can you:

(1) Survey a range of source materials and select what is important, recognising and rejecting unsuitable approaches?
(2) Organise your materials into a sensible and logical order?
(3) Write and rewrite the material into a new coherent whole?
(4) Produce the required number of words?
(5) Finish your writing on time?

In the cold, hard world of work, if your writing is seriously flawed, or in the wrong genre or tone, or late, or too long or too short, you won't get paid, or at best won't be offered more work. In the cold, hard world of the exam, you'll be given a research folder and a week to prepare, then you'll have 2 hours and 30 minutes to write a 1,000-word first draft and a commentary.

In both contexts, the criteria are essentially the same: is the text usable? Does it follow the instructions given? Does it engage its audience in a lively and appropriate way, so that the audience would actually read it? If the answer to these questions is yes, you'll get paid — or high marks.

Text types and genres

Editorial writing demands a capacity to write in specialised text types and genres. To develop this skill you must study a variety of examples of texts as style models and practise writing in these specialised ways. This section of the guide outlines the main text types and genres that are set in Unit 5 exams and gives examples from past papers.

Before continuing it is worth distinguishing between 'text types' and 'genres', because these terms are sometimes used interchangeably. 'Text type' refers to the format of the text and its material presence: where you would see the text and what physical form it would take — for example, whether it is in a book, a script for a radio programme, a display board or web page. 'Genre' means what the writer is using the text to achieve; examples include an informative text, a marketing text and a set of educational materials. A set of educational materials, for instance, might take the form of a book, a display board or a web page.

The distinction is worth making because not all text types are the same. Just because something is written for radio does not mean that it should be like Radio 1, Radio 5 or Radio 4. When preparing for editorial writing you should have experience of text types in a range of genres — that is to say, written in relation to different profiles of audience, purpose and context.

Tone of voice

Getting the tone right is more important than specialised conventions. Remember that Unit 5 is an English Language exam and tests your ability to write powerfully and appropriately, using standard English. Achieving an accurate tone and style is more important than knowing the detailed conventions of specialised text types. In the case of some text types, such as radio scripts, there is no single set of such conventions anyway.

Magazines and newspapers

There is a tendency among some students to see magazine and newspaper writing as the 'safe option' among the various editorial writing tasks set. This is because in many ways the printed page is a more familiar format than writing for the spoken mode, or for more modern formats associated with computer technology, such as websites. Put simply, we see more newspapers and magazines than radio scripts in life, and you are likely to have written something for a magazine in your AS coursework. However, despite this apparent familiarity, it is necessary to look closely at magazines and newspapers in terms of their register and discourse structure.

Note that magazine-style writing can be required by other, non-magazine tasks. The task requiring candidates to write a Glastonbury CD booklet essentially demanded this journalistic style, but candidates had to remember that they were writing for something that would ultimately end up as a 13 cm × 13 cm booklet.

Features of the genre

Before you begin to construct your 1,000-word answer, you will need to be aware of audience and purpose, as well as the context and the conventions of the genre.

Pragmatics

When writing for a specific audience, **pragmatics** come into play: the writer implies shared interests, cultural understanding or lifestyle with the reader. Assumptions about ideology and lifestyle will be reflected in the style and point of view of the writing, also known as the **bias**. It is essential that you get the tone of the article right to reflect this perceived relationship, otherwise you could end up alienating your readers.

Clues in the question

As always, the first stage in determining the style and pragmatic approach to adopt is to read the question carefully and identify the subtleties of the task you have been set. The following question is from the June 2004 paper:

> A magazine aimed at parents entitled *You and Your Child* is running a series of articles on key topics in modern education.
> The articles are intended to cover topics in a lively and interesting way and also to provide reassuring advice about how parents can help their children in these areas.
> You have been asked to write the article on spelling using the material in the source file.
> Write about 1,000 words.
> Briefly and clearly indicate your preferred layout, as well as any illustrations that you wish to be used.
> Your text should be accompanied by a commentary in which you explain some of the significant decisions and choices you have made in writing it. The commentary should be approximately 150–200 words.

There are some clear clues in this question. Your task is to inform in a lively and interesting way, and to be reassuring. Your audience is made up of parents — probably proud parents who want to get it right, if they go to the trouble of buying a parenting magazine.

Choose the right tone

Deciding on the tone of your article is one of the key judgements you will have to make. Read how previous examinees, answering the *You and Your Child* question, got the tone wrong:

> Parental influence can have a big effect on how successful your children are in their spelling. Perhaps you were rubbish at spelling when you were at school and you have passed your fear on to your child.

This is hardly reassuring, and certain to inspire guilt rather than confidence. Another examinee was patronising and overfamiliar:

> All you have to say is 'i before e except after c, when its an 'ee' sound'. Simple, isn't it? Easy peasy. You could say it along with your child and learn to spell together.

The following example is defeatist and overemphasises the difficulties:

> Spelling is an extremely difficult skill because the English spelling system is so complex. Don't expect your child to be good at it as nobody else is.

A common problem is writing in an overcomplex way by using source material without sufficient rewriting for the needs of the audience. This is a frequent comment in exam reports.

Newspapers and magazines cover a continuum from serious and formal styles, such as in *The Lancet* and *Birds*, to informal and/or humorous styles, such as in *Hello!* and *FHM*. The tone must fit both the subject and the audience. **Serious and formal writing** will feature accurate standard English and greater complexity at a lexical level. **Informal styles** will feature some non-standard grammar, pseudo-intimacy (i.e. mock conversation, more use of the second person pronoun), and lexically they might include informal vocabulary, slang and possibly mild taboo language. It is difficult to generalise too much, which makes getting it right in the exam a challenge. Generally, the more specialised and motivated the reader, the fewer graphological and discourse 'helpers' you need. Conversely, if the reader is general and casual, the more varied and accessible your layout needs to be.

Signposting

Everyone uses signposting when they write. Discourse features such as sentences and paragraphs are signposts that are common to most writing, as they indicate changes of topic — but you are never going to write an essay in this exam. Discourse features in magazines and newspapers, such as headings, subheadings, breakers and teasers, show what the topic of the next section is. As soon as you open a magazine or newspaper, you will see discourse features — columns are an obvious example that you can include in your layout sketch if required. It is worth browsing through different publications to see the different techniques.

How much signposting to use

It is easy when writing for magazines and newspapers to fall into the trap of using the repetitive formula of heading/paragraph/heading/paragraph. This pattern works effectively with highly motivated readers, such as the audience for *You and Your Child*, and hopefully you reading this book. But if your readers are casual or not as motivated, you will have to work harder at the way you use graphological features and layout, and in your variation of grammatical structures (first person, second person, third person viewpoints).

As an example, take the following task, which came up in the 2002 summer exam and was based on the 'Gateshead Quays' source material pack:

> A national railway company produces a magazine which promotes destinations served by its trains. It is available free to passengers.
> You have been asked to write an article on the regeneration of the Gateshead Quays which will encourage a wide variety of people to visit the area. You should pay particular attention to the Baltic Centre, the Millennium Bridge and the Music Centre, but you may include anything else from the source material you consider suitable.

The question indicates that passengers receive the magazine for free as they travel (and so do not have to part with hard-earned cash for the privilege of reading it), so the target audience for this article is wide. We are also told that the article needs to appeal to 'a wide variety of people'. To suit such a broad and less-motivated audience, the writing needs to be accessible and well signposted, with no unnecessary technical terms, and a common lexical field. The subject is highly visual, so lots of photographs (drawn from the resource pack) are essential. The audience can be assumed to be largely an adult one, given the context and genre of the magazine. The readers probably picked up the magazine because they were bored, and are likely to be reading it aboard potentially crowded, noisy or busy trains. The article therefore needs to be easy to follow; clear labelling of the main features (the Baltic Centre, the Music Centre and the Millennium Bridge) would be a bare minimum.

Audience and purpose

When you incorporate appropriate discourse features into your magazine or newspaper text, you are gaining marks under AO2, which requires you to 'demonstrate expertise and accuracy in writing for a variety of specific purposes and audiences'. A combination of the right register and discourse markers, and a clear focus on your audience, will lead to success.

The words 'promote' and 'encourage' in the Gateshead Quays question seem to identify a purely persuasive purpose for this task. However, candidates who fell back on the techniques for persuasive writing learned in class (and peppered their writing with strongly emotive language, an overt use of direct address, lots of phonetic effects, the 'rule of three' etc.) actually lost marks for misreading purpose and tone. Why?

To answer this question, we can refer to the mark scheme used by examiners to identify strengths and weaknesses in students' work. This states that:

> The reader should be persuaded, but in a subtle way with an authorial voice combining a degree of objectivity with enthusiasm. Too obvious a persuasive voice would be less effective.

The best texts, which made it into the 51–60 mark bracket, were identified as 'creating a voice that convincingly persuades with due regard to the reader's intelligence'. In the case of the Gateshead Quays task, the voice or tone of the writing is closely bound up with a consideration of audience and a careful attention to the subtleties of purpose — after all, it is likely that the majority of people reading the magazine will be doing so simply to pass the time, and they may find it an insult to their intelligence to be given a complimentary magazine which is too obviously an advertisement to promote the railway company and its destinations. This is an article, not an advertisement, and so the persuasive purpose has to be tempered with informative content to interest the readers in the regeneration of Gateshead (factual objectivity, rather than an obvious bias), and even mildly entertaining elements (this would strike an 'enthusiastic' tone).

Other techniques

WOBs, BOTs, boxes and grammatical variety

WOB and BOT are printers' jargon for 'white on black' and 'black on tan'. WOBs and BOTs can make headings or separate areas of text stand out. Some texts are super-imposed over a background picture. Of course, in the exam you should not try to create this effect — just indicate what you want in your layout sketch.

One area of a subject can be isolated in a separate box. This technique is often used in gossipy magazines for 'My Personal Hell'-style features. There is an added advantage to doing this: you can change to a first-person narrative, which adds variety, and gives you something to discuss in your commentary.

A section in a separate box for the *You and Your Child* spelling task, entitled 'How I helped my child become a competent speller' would attract the audience. Using the first person adds authenticity and builds trust with the reader. The second person is also worth using as it draws the reader in — for example, 'Why you should visit the arts centre'. Questions are a useful feature, particularly in headings, such as 'What's so clever about the Millennium Bridge?'

Lists and A–Zs

You are sure to have noticed how popular lists and A–Z guides have become in the media. (Note that A–Z guides can be trickier to complete under exam conditions.) A section entitled 'Top five features of the Millennium Bridge' or 'Five astonishing facts about the Millennium Bridge' is more accessible to the reader than the same information in an unlabelled paragraph.

Layout

Finally, briefly and clearly indicate your preferred layout if this is asked for. (Note the signposting of the word 'finally'. This is the last bit.) Some candidates draw the magazine layout painstakingly, then try to cram in all the text. This is difficult, time-consuming and definitely not necessary. Indicate the layout in a quick sketch, like the one below for the Glastonbury CD booklet task. Be sure to label clearly the writing that you want to go in the Text 1 and Text 2 positions.

Picture D from p. 4 of source pack — 'The year of mud'		Picture E — aerial shot of the Tor	Picture H — close up from p. 9 of Michael Eavis
		Picture C — the pyramid stage	
Glastonbury now and then			
Picture A — Oasis	**Text 1 in two columns**	**Text 2 in three columns**	

Unusual genres

As you can see from the list on pp. 74–76 of tasks and genres set by AQA, there are many possible styles and formats. As a student you need to develop skills in these varied ways of writing. The next few pages introduce some of the more unusual genres that have been set in past exams: web pages, display boards and radio scripts. You will be shown how to prepare to write in these formats.

But before looking at the three specialist genres you should take note of two warnings. First, the three genres that follow are just three examples of what is asked for. You need to practise writing effectively in at least six or seven different genres.

Second, there is no need to be too concerned with learning the design conventions for these different genres. Most of the marks available are for creating a cohesive piece of writing that seamlessly weaves together source material with a linking authorial voice. Examiners will want to know if the text is written in an appropriate style and tone — layout is secondary.

Web pages

The internet is a new publishing opportunity for everyone. On average 30,000 pages are added each day. Of course, these are not all wonderful. As Homer Simpson says: 'The internet. What treasures! We can learn what some nerd thinks about *Star Trek*.' But there is also fascinating information. For the purposes of your Unit 5 exam you need to show awareness of features of the genre and to be able to organise your information appropriately.

Note that writing the design for a web page by hand in an exam hall is a constrained activity by comparison with creating it on a computer. The examiner will credit your use of language and your discourse structure. There will be little credit for the artistic quality of handcrafted fonts and homemade images.

Features of the genre

Web pages must consider 'attention economy', in which all websites compete for the attention of potential users. They have three key properties that mark them out from the other types of writing task:

(1) In real life they are constituted as screen text over static paper copy: reading screen text makes different demands from reading from the page.
(2) They have multi-modality of form: written text can be combined with images, sound files and video clips. Writing web pages involves designing an ensemble of communication in which various modes can be mixed and matched.
(3) Their interactivity arises from the hypertext discourse structure, in which text is not sequenced in a linear manner, but by discourse chunks that are linked electronically. The reader or user remakes the text by his/her choice of links, rather than by reading from the beginning to the end in a linear fashion.

After each exam series AQA publishes an exam report summarising the strengths and weaknesses in student answers. The report for the 'Codes and ciphers' web-page task read:

> [The task] stretched able candidates and provided them with an opportunity to show their control over the source material by reorganising it into the complex cross patterns of the genre of web pages. The most successful scripts showed excellent awareness of web conventions such as animated gifs, hyperlinks, sound files and discussion boxes where readers could add their views on the site.
>
> The least successful scripts made no attempt to replicate web conventions, and, indeed, it was not until the commentary was read that examiners were able to tell that the scripts had been meant as web pages.　　　　　　　　　　　　　　(June 2002)

The 'Codes and ciphers' question asked candidates to 'introduce the general public to the fascinating world of language'. Clearly this implies an interested and lively tone. The question that you should keep asking yourself is: 'How effective would the script be for its intended user?'

Pragmatics

Reading words on screen is harder than reading from the page. Screen flicker, dry eyes and a fixed viewing point mean that books have a definite advantage: you can stick a book mark in at the point you stop reading, go for a walk taking the book with you, pick it up again when lying in bed, and find your place instantly. Searching for errors in a text is easier on a printout — screen reading is more difficult. As a web writer you need to take account of these differences.

Although web pages are not suitable for lengthy reading, they have advantages over printed text in other respects. The topics are more clearly structured and subdivided. Menu bars and scrolling make finding key information a speedier task, and search engines make it possible to track down the information you need much more quickly.

Web pages have a flexible structure and 'chunking' — short paragraphs and clear labelling. Their non-linear structure means you can jump around the pages (i.e. you don't have to start at 'a' and work your way through to 'z').

Your design must take advantage of these factors. Indeed, the concept of **links** is a crucial feature in web texts, and understanding how these work is essential to writing high-quality digital text.

Writing good web pages

Orientation, the linguist William Labov's phrase for knowing where you are, is vital in web writing. The audience needs to know how to find its way in, around and out of a document, and how to quickly get back to the main menu page. This is often done through devices that appear on every page, such as the **menu bar**, or the simple '**return to main menu**' button.

Studying different examples of web pages is a good idea, but bear in mind that anyone can write and publish unedited text on the internet. Some pages are poorly organised and written and do little more than transfer a written text onto the screen. You can do better than that, and you will be highly rewarded in the exam if you put thought and expertise into your text and make good use of the conventions of the genre.

Good web pages have the following features:
- **Clear orientation.** Main subject areas are at the top of the web page and arranged as entrance points to the interior pages. This can also be done through a strip down the side or across the bottom of the page called a **navigation bar**.
- **Brevity.** It is even more important to cut every word that does not pay its way. A single screen should never have more than 200 words. Subdivide before you write anything longer than this.
- **Chunking.** Paragraph breaks refresh dry eyes and provide a stopping point so that the reader can rest and decide whether he/she needs or wants to go on.
- **Short sentences.** Keep sentences to a single clause. Write in the active voice and use one idea per sentence. Never write sentences that are longer than 20 words.
- **Simple vocabulary.** Use plain, specific words wherever possible.
- **Be direct.** Address your audience as 'you'. Use 'we' to talk about yourself or the organisation you are writing for.
- **Links and search facilities.** Many web pages have useful hyperlinks to other web pages on similar themes, or may incorporate a search engine so that you can find information quickly within the site.

Audience

Thinking about your audience will decide the pragmatics of your page. Who is the audience and how and why is it reading your pages?

The audience for web pages is extremely varied and may be searching your pages for a whole range of purposes. You have to respond by making your pages accessible, friendly and, most important of all, *well organised*. Your readers may be interested in only 10% of your page, so you've got to make it easy to find that 10%. The need for good menus, well-planned pages and clear links make this a genre that demands careful planning.

Display boards

Display boards are common features at country parks, stately homes, zoos and museums. Let's take as an example a display board at a country park. People read it to:
- find out where they are
- find directions to the main attractions and features
- read about the history of the park
- find the nearest place that offers shelter and a cup of tea

- read about the wildlife
- see how to get back to the car park
- settle an argument
- find out specialist information

There are probably more possible reasons than these. As a display-board writer you have to make your material accessible, readable, well organised and clearly signposted so that all of your possible readers can quickly find the information they want. Some will read all of the display board, whereas others will simply look for the information they need.

Signposting

Whatever your display board is used for, it must have clear signposting. Use the features common to magazines, wall displays and textbooks:

- headings, subheadings and side bars
- topic boxes
- bullet points
- illustrations
- numbered points
- lists (sometimes in alphabetical order)
- glossaries

Maps and line drawings are typical features. It is worth looking at some display boards, such as indoor information boards in museums and outdoor guides. Here is a typical, and real, example of a display board overlooking a river estuary:

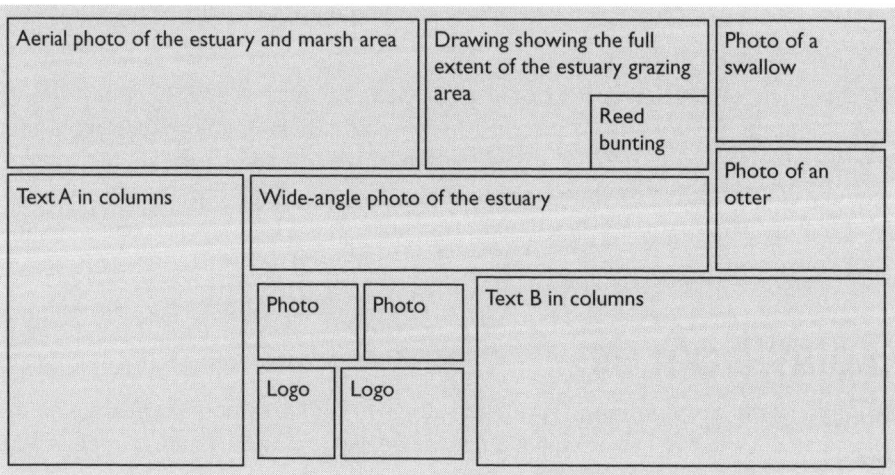

You need to adopt a method like this when the question asks you to indicate your preferred layout. Draw a labelled diagram to show the arrangement of the different elements, then write Text A and Text B separately. Add a key or guide for the photos and drawings you use — this will save a lot of time.

Examples

Below is Text A in its 'raw' state. Put yourself in the examiner's shoes. Read it carefully as it includes mistakes. Ask yourself: 'Does it suit its likely audiences and their needs?' Think about the following frameworks and relate them to the purpose and context of the text:

- lexis
- semantics
- discourse structure
- grammar
- pragmatics
- graphology

Text A

The view across the Neath Estuary of the grazing marsh may not be the prettiest landscape you have studied. However grazing marshes have been lost to development and barrage schemes around the UK at such a rate that they are now a UK priority habitat and the Neath marsh is surprisingly the third largest relatively undamaged floodplain left in Wales.

These floodplain marshes are unique because they are periodically flooded by brackish (salty) water. This would wipe out the majority of plants but the salt marsh plants you will find along the Neath Estuary are specially adapted to cope with regular drowning in salt water. Some of these plants are shown in the display. **Sea milkwort** (*Glaux maritima*) and **sea aster** (*Aster tripolium*), have fleshy leaves in which to retain fresh water, others like the strange looking **glasswort** (*Salicornia*) have the swollen, succulent stems and branches.

As its name suggests glasswort was once used in the manufacture of glass and there are references to its use for glass and soap in the Bible. **English scurvygrass** (*Cochlearia anglice*) another fairly typical species of the Neath Estuary is, unlike its name suggests, in fact, a member of the cabbage family. It is a rich source of vitamin C and was used to prevent scurvy among sailors – the leaves were even used a beer called scurvygrass ale! **Lesser centaury** (*Centaureum pulchella*), which is also found on the grazing marsh, is known for its healing properties and an infusion from it has long been used as a tonic to aid digestion; as far back as Saxon times herbalists prescribed it for 'snake bites and other poisons'.

Flood plain grazing marshes are not only important because of their plants. This habitat is important for birds. Among the species often seen along the Neath Estuary is the **goosander** (*Mergus merganser*). A member of the duck family, this fish-eating bird first bred in Wales in 1970 and likes to breed on fast flowing rivers, most frequently in holes and trees. Look out for the males distinctive green head.

Small groups of native **lapwings** (*Vanellus vanellum*) may be seen here, breeding on the ground in the spring. Now one of the three most endangered birds in Wales, they were once a common sight in Glamorgan. Larger flocks may appear in the winter months but

> these are visiting European lapwings. The local decline is probably due to the increased use of pesticides (which kill their food) and improved drainage practices decreasing the wet grassland areas they prefer. They have a distinctive flight and pee-wit call after which they are sometimes called.
>
> Due to a loss of suitable nesting habitat caused by development along the Neath Port Talbot coastal belt, and despite the possibility of flooding, lapwings have started to attempt breed here.

An examiner marking this text would start by weighing up the good and bad points:

Good points
- The Latin lexis is there for the specialist, showing an awareness of a dual audience.
- Some meanings are glossed.
- The information is structured into paragraphs and divided into two.
- The writer sounds as though he/she knows the material.

Bad points
- Lexically the text shows a strong carryover from textbooks and source material.
- The sentence structure is complex, with long, multi-clausal (and sometimes inaccurate) sentences, with inaccurate standard English grammar.
- For a general audience some lexis could be simplified or made more concrete (e.g. drainage practices, suitable nesting habitat, infusion).
- The discourse structure and graphology could be more successfully integrated (e.g. giving photos of species alongside the information about them).
- The display board is not interesting or lively enough to maintain audience interest, given the outdoor context (it may be raining/cold, lots of other distractions etc.).

An examiner would then ask: how successful is this document? How well does it fulfil its intended purpose?

How can the text be improved?
The text can be improved simply and in a number of ways:
(1) Lexically, some of the more difficult words and phrases can be shortened and simplified.
(2) Semantically, the information can be more immediately linked to relevant pictures. Topic boxes could be used for birds and plants.
(3) Bullets and numbered points would make the information more attractive and readable.
(4) Using headings would make a major difference. Readers could skim down to the section that interests them without having to plough through unwanted information.
(5) Greater links between the information and the context would enliven the material. If readers were invited to look for patches of sea aster and scurvywort to their left, or for a place marked on the map, then interactivity and interest would be improved.

Text B is reproduced below. It has its original justification and layout to give you a clearer idea of how it actually looked. There are errors in the standard English grammar. Texts A and B together total 813 words, about 200 short of the standard case-study length. It is vital to get used to what 1,000 words of text look like.

Text B

Reed buntings (*Emberiza schienicus*) are associated with reed beds, riverbanks and marshy areas and are found all year round in the small patches of reeds on the left. They have a characteristic black head and white 'moustache' and like the tall phagmites reed (these are Britain's tallest grass) to roost in. These birds are also nationally in decline, possibly due to the deterioration and loss of their habitats and changes in agricultural practices.

A local favourite the **mute swan** (*Cygnus olad*) often frequents the Estuary and canal system. Mute swans are present throughout Britain and prefer still or sluggish water and a supply of aquatic vegetation for food. The male (or cob) defends its territories aggressively against intruders while the female (or pen) incubates their eggs (usually 4–7) on a nest made on a mound.

Swallows (*Hirundo rustica*) arrive from their winter in southern Africa in the spring, with the adults usually returning to the same breeding site as previous years. When they arrive at the estuary they will have flown more than 6,000 miles. They feed on insects caught on the wing and swoop down to drink from water. In the autumn the birds once again fly south, although it was once thought that they buried themselves in the mud of rivers and ponds for the winter!

Otters (*Lutra lutra*) are one of the largest carnivores and, after suffering declines in the 1950s and 1960s, are now making a significant recovery locally having returned to the Tawe, Dulais and Neath rivers. Others are semi-aquatic and use all types of wetland habitat including the grazing marsh, canal and Neath Estuary. They defend their home ranges and are thought to kill the mink that have spread along the rivers and streams. Ideally they need unpolluted water in which to hunt and undisturbed areas on the banks to lie up during the day and as a place to breed.

If you see any unusual wildlife or large numbers of particular birds on the estuary please contact **Neath Port Talbot Biodiversity Forum** (01234 567891) as they will be grateful for your information.

Examiner response

- **Deictic and contextual reference.** There is clear understanding of the context of both the river in front of the notice, and the photographs and diagrams on the display board; 'with reed beds, riverbanks and marshy areas and are found all year round in the small patches of reeds on the left' directs the reader to the location of what is being referred to.
- **Interactivity.** The text shows consideration for the readers and creates links with

them: 'A local favourite the **mute swan**...'; 'If you see any unusual wildlife or large numbers of particular birds on the estuary...'.

- **Variety of lexis.** The range of lexis is broad to suit a wide-ranging audience. For the expert, there are Latin and specialist terms ('**Swallows** (*Hirundo rustica*)', 'phagmites reed'); for the layperson there is less technical language ('They defend their home ranges and are thought to kill the mink that have spread along the rivers and streams'). Notice the variation in lexis from the polysyllabic, Latinate terms to the monosyllabic, Anglo-Saxon vocabulary.
- **Coordinate sentences.** These make reading and understanding easier: 'Mute swans are present throughout Britain and prefer still or sluggish water and a supply of aquatic vegetation for food'.
- **Uncomplicated discourse structure.** The lexis in bold act as signposts. While Text B is easier to read and scan than Text A, there is room for improvement in making the display board easy to use.

Radio scripts

Writing a radio script is a task that you may have tried in your AS original writing work. It is an interesting challenge and has its own particular demands. It is worth thinking about the contextual and pragmatic features of this aural format, because these have a profound influence on the way you choose and structure language.

Sound texts

Sound texts on radio are carefully planned and edited. Radio shows and programmes are not allowed to overrun their time or to be too short. What may sound like a spontaneous programme to you has probably been edited. Talk Radio's phone-in shows might allow spontaneous talk from the callers, but it is carefully controlled. The host of the show has the option of cutting off speakers if they are boring, repetitive or obscene.

The majority of radio programmes are carefully edited in a sound studio. *Most are not live.* A programme like 'Oasis: What's the Story?' (see the extract reproduced on p. 25) is made up from a wide range of interviews and pre-recorded clips that are edited together. The opening 'banter' between Noel and Liam is made up of selected highlights (or lowlights) and may even consist of material from several interviews that has been reordered. The other 11 voices in the programme are all integrated into a new narrative controlled by the producers and the host, Mark Radcliffe. Add in the skilful use of appropriate music tracks faded up and down to punctuate the verbal clips, and you have a carefully controlled piece of writing.

So, the creation of a radio programme such as this mirrors exactly the process you go through in an editorial writing exam — creating a new piece of text from a variety of sources. Clearly a lot of material was rejected in the creation of this programme, just as you must reject or rewrite unsuitable material to satisfy the needs of your audience.

'Oasis: What's the Story?'

Script (first 4 minutes)	FX	Approximate timing (seconds)
LINK: This is Radio 2 and the time is 8 p.m. It's time for 'Oasis: What's the Story?', introduced by Mark Radcliffe.		
MARK RADCLIFFE: Hello, I'm Mark Radcliffe. The following programme contains strong language, which although we've beeped it out, may offend some listeners, so sorry.		10
This is Noel Gallagher from Oasis and what you are about to hear is the story of a band from Manchester.	'Rock and Roll Star'	75
LIAM: This is the best band in the world I think personally.	Fade up	5
NOEL: We didn't form, you know, we exploded. We just came and that was it.		
LIAM: We've got passion, know what I mean, I'm just mad for it.		
NOEL: Well, everybody better start giving me thanks and praise now, because I, in fact, rule.		
LIAM: He's the b*(beep)*ks as a song writer.	Fade up	5
NOEL: This is the truth on this day, and on this day only, because as you're listening to this, things have probably changed. Have I just contradicted myself? I think I did, didn't I. But I'm allowed to do that because I'm a Gemini, see?	Fade up	15
NOEL: We give you this, we hope you find it funny, first and foremost, because, it's supposed to be funny.		
LIAM: I'm gonna break your f*(beep)*in' nose man.	'Free to Do Whatever I Want'	
NOEL: Laugh at the people involved and laugh at the stories.		

LIAM: Shut up. Will you shut up a minute, right, songwriter.		
NOEL: Shut the *(beep)* up, man. *(To listeners)* Don't be too offended by the swearing.		
LIAM: I love him, he's top, but he pisses me off and I piss him off.		
NOEL: It's just the way that we are, y'know.		
LIAM: I think he does it because he's a *(beep)* full stop.		
NOEL: Thank you very much.	Fade up chorus	15
MARK RADCLIFFE: Hello and welcome to 'Oasis: What's the Story?', the true and unexpurgated tale of the biggest band Britain has produced in the last 10 years, and the two brothers at its helm. I'm Mark Radcliffe and over the next 60 minutes we'll be hearing of drugs, drink, debauchery, assault with a cricket bat and an awful lot of swearing. So, if you're offended by this sound *(beep)* then I can only apologise up-front. You *(beep)*. The Oasis story begins in the northwest in the early 90s. Noel and Liam Gallagher, the two youngest brothers in a Manchester Irish family, grew up in Burnage, a not especially desirable area of the city. Despite artistic leanings, Noel kept them hidden from his mates.		
NOEL: Out of all the people that we knocked about with I was the only person that could play a musical instrument and I kept that quite quiet because if you were artistic in any way they would almost label you homosexual. Not that there's anything wrong with that you understand, but it was not a very laddish thing to be doing, sitting playing acoustic guitar, you know, while everyone else was out robbing houses and stuff, so I kept it quite quiet but Liam thought I was very strange for a few years.	Fade up	5

Audience

Your audience is likely to be varied. Some listeners will be dedicated fans of the programme, listening to every word in their bedrooms. Some will be driving their cars, listening when they can spare the attention. Others will be casual listeners who have switched on the radio to listen while doing something else — washing up, potting plants or painting.

Your listeners can tune in part way through the programme or can have their attention distracted by a visitor, the phone ringing or a call of nature. The meaning of your text must survive all these eventualities.

Features of the genre

The beauty of radio is that pure sounds can take you anywhere in space and time. A few words and a sound effect can tell you that you have travelled back 1,000 years, or gone to an exotic location, or journeyed into outer space. This means you have to orientate your audience regularly. Other features of the genre are that you will often use a variety of voices and a link person to hold the programme together.

Orientation

Tell your listeners **where** they are, **when** the events are taking place and **who** is speaking. In a written text you can go back and check information if you miss it the first time; in a spoken text this is not possible, so you have to guard against your audience getting lost.

Looking at the Oasis script shows how orientation is achieved:
- Through the music, which most Radio 2 listeners will recognise.
- Through the Manchester accents and voices.
- Through the repetition of the name Oasis.
- More explicitly when Mark Radcliffe comes in after 2 minutes of Noel and Liam talking and tells us exactly what we are listening to, why Oasis is important, who the main band members are and what we will hear in the next 60 minutes.
- After 20 minutes of the programme Mark Radcliffe makes the following announcement: 'My name's Mark Radcliffe and this is 'Oasis: What's the Story?' on BBC Radio 2, 88–91 FM. For mystified listeners Mark Radcliffe was the link voice — comparable to an anchorman or woman on television — an important role in radio.

The link voice: someone to hold onto

The first 20 minutes of the Oasis programme included the voices of Noel Gallagher, Liam Gallagher, Paul 'Bonehead' Arthurs, Tim Abbott, Marcus Russell, Daniella Suavey, Paulo Hewitt, Damon Minchella, Richard Ashcroft and Dougie Payne. In the full hour dozens of different sources and voices were knitted together into a programme. It would be easy to lose track of what was happening and what the sequence was if there was not some calm at the centre of the storm. This is the role of the link voice, or the anchorman or woman (sometimes both).

The link voice keeps the listeners on track and orientated, and carries them from sound segment to sound segment, maintaining the narrative thread. A newsreader does much the same job, telling the audience when the subject has changed, and giving some solid ground to stand on. 'Oasis: What's the Story?' used different speakers and contributors, but Mark Radcliffe kept the programme in order by using linking comments such as these:

MARK RADCLIFFE: Journalist Paolo Hewitt, who wrote the sleeve notes to 'What's the Story Morning Glory?', witnessed the band's attraction first hand.

PAOLO HEWITT: They had that thing which all good groups need.

Sometimes Mark Radcliffe both introduced and sequenced the contributors' voices, never allowing the audience to lose track of who was talking about the band:

MARK RADCLIFFE: And it wasn't just paying punters who were enthralled. Damon Minchella from Ocean Colour Scene, and first Richard Ashcroft, at that time lead singer of The Verve:

RICHARD ASHCROFT: I clearly, vividly, remember the first time we saw them, I think it was Wolverhampton. I just walked into the hall and they were sound checking and I just sort of stared at Liam for about 10 minutes and he stared at me and we just stared each other out like.

DAMON MINCHELLA: My first reaction to seeing them live was like it was Liam totally, and the rest of the band just stood there and didn't do anything.

Redundancy

Because the spoken word is such a temporary phenomenon we build into all spoken texts what is known technically as **redundancy**. Put simply, information is repeated. If you look at the last quotes from Ashcroft and Minchella you'll see the repetition of ideas ('clearly, vividly'; 'I just sort of stared at Liam...and he stared at me...and we just stared each other out') and implied meaning ('it was Liam totally', i.e. it was Liam who made an impression).

You have probably noticed that your teachers tend to repeat important ideas two or three times in different ways. On radio, several hundred listeners will have tuned in at any one time, so orientating devices and redundancy need to be built into your scripts.

Other styles of script

Of course, 'Oasis: What's the Story?' is one particular type of radio script: the music documentary. Its structure — short 'teasers', followed by an orientating statement, then a chronological account of the band's rise to fame — is typical of music documentaries and radio programmes, but not the only possible approach. On p. 29 is an extract another script, this time from Radio 4.

Script	FX
ANNOUNCER: But before then it's time for *The Serendipity of Science*. In this last programme in the series, Simon Singh finds out about the surprising number of breakthroughs which have happened by accident, in 'From Venom to Viagra'.	Background 'New Age' music
MALE IRISH VOICE: All of the very exciting discoveries in science have rarely been achieved by systematic scientific study. More often than not they have been serendipitous.	
1ST MALE US VOICE: It was a wonderful, err, moment of light, err, excitement, and I felt at that point that what was before me could be the source of the discovery of something useful.	
2ND MALE US VOICE: That's the nice thing about science, once in a while you find something you think no one else has seen before. And that's a good feeling.	Fade out
SIMON SINGH: The moment of discovery must be an extraordinary experience, especially when it's totally unexpected, when there's an element of luck. (Pause) And one field which has had more than its fair share of luck is medicine. Many new drugs have been accidental discoveries. My first tale of medical serendipity begins in 1908, when a group of commercial flower growers called on two Chicago botanists, William Crocker and Lee Knight, for some help.	
RP VOICE: They were approached by carnation growers in the neighbouring state of Wisconsin, who were losing money because they sent their flowers down to Chicago and they were put in a greenhouse, and they found that the petals that were open would close, that the buds that were about to open didn't open, seedlings died, and in some cases leaves began to curl up. So they asked them to look into the properties of the illuminating gas in the greenhouse and they identified the toxic element as ethylene in the mixture.	
SIMON SINGH: The ethylene was so toxic that even minute traces would damage plants, a finding which William Crocker casually mentioned to friends during a late-night game of cards. Medic Arno Luckhart was at the table and it struck him that ethylene might also be harmful to humans. He tested ethylene on rats, but instead of killing them it merely sent them to sleep. He wondered if he had stumbled on a new anaesthetic and decided to try it on humans. Peter Drury from the History of Anaesthesia Society:	

PETER DRURY: He started off by inhaling it himself with a student colleague. The student was called Carter, a medical student, he had to go first because he was unmarried, apparently, and literally they just inhaled it for a minute or so, holding their mask in one hand and the other arm up in the air, and when the arm dropped the mask was taken off and then he got more volunteers and gradually increased the length of time for which ethylene was breathed, and by about 1922 he felt ready to give a demonstration to the anaesthetists at the Presbyterian hospital in Chicago.	
RP VOICE: Experiment three. The authors tried out on themselves the immediate effect of the gas, then further subjects volunteered and were anaesthetised far past the stage of analgesia, for in two, NK and ACS, the safety pin was pushed through the skin without provoking reflex movement of the arm, much less sensation of pain in the subjects. ACS laughed a great deal before complete anaesthetisation, on recovery he talked excitedly and incoherently of his experience. NK, while recovering from the anaesthetic but while still dazed, vomited up a large breakfast he had taken several hours before. He had no recollection of having vomited. Nausea was not experienced and the subject ate a hearty meal within the hour.	Fade up slow cello music

There are a few points to note about this extract:
- The orientation functions carried out by the announcer and the link voice.
- The sparing use of effects to set a mood.
- The variety of voices used (though all are male).
- The human details that make the story interesting. Remember that the majority of case-study tasks will be narratives, though their purposes will vary.
- The tricky spellings. It does not build confidence in the examiner if you misspell words that are spelled correctly in the sources. Be careful.

Don't script the unscriptable

Sometimes candidates try to enliven their scripts by attempting to script 'live' radio chat. You cannot write a script for a spontaneous discussion or for a phone-in. Live radio is completely different. No one turns up for a live discussion with their script prepared beforehand, complete with hesitations, repetitions and pauses. That is to mistake the nature of the programme. If you look back at the opening of the Oasis documentary, it appears that Mark Radcliffe is chairing an informal chat with the Gallaghers. However, if you listen to the programme many times, it becomes clear that Mark Radcliffe recorded his linking pieces separately (and probably never met the Gallaghers). Noel and Liam's 'off-the-cuff' remarks were taken from an unstructured (but recorded) interview, then edited together afterwards with Mark Radcliffe's comments to make a coherent piece. If you look at the transcript carefully the adjacency pairs break some of Grice's maxims of relevance, and that is because the apparent conversation is a patchwork of edited material. So, whatever you do in a radio piece, *don't have an interviewer introducing an informal chat with some guests.*

Preparing the pre-release materials

Students sometimes say that the editorial writing materials they are given in Unit 5 are difficult and dull, and that the writing tasks do not relate to the kinds of reading and listening they prefer. To some extent, this is deliberate: the materials are designed to be complex and challenging, and without a preparation method you may well find them difficult and chaotic. The writing tasks model some of the common types of writing used in professional contexts, such as journalism, broadcasting, digital media authoring and public relations, and not the writing styles that appeal most to students.

Unit 5 models the kind of writing experience people encounter in their working lives, where a complex set of sources has to be studied, sifted and summarised, so that it can be redeployed for a new purpose, audience and context. People expect such writing to be engaging, or they may not bother to read it. Your role is to organise the complex and chaotic source material so it can be reused easily in new contexts.

What you will get

You will be given two sets of source materials on different topics. *Don't* discard one set because you don't like the look of it. After all, as a professional writer you can be commissioned (and paid) to do all kinds of writing.

These sets of materials will contain between 12 and 20 different articles in a variety of styles for different audiences. Each article will have its source included on it somewhere. Some sources are used more than once, as you will soon see, and the ordering is random. You will have 20–30 pages of information in each set of source materials.

What you must do

Your overall purpose is to turn thousands of words of source materials into approximately 1,000 words of text **that is suited to a new audience and purpose**. Time is not really a problem as you have 2 hours 30 minutes — only 400 words an hour (or six words a minute). Easy. The difficulty lies in rewriting the sources as a new text for a new audience, and choosing the right register for the new purpose that you have been given.

To write a new text, you need to be able to access the source materials so that they suit your purpose, audience and context. To access the materials in this way, you need to be familiar with them, so that they are at your fingertips.

If you do not familiarise yourself with the source materials, it is likely that *they* will write your answer and push you out of control. You will include texts from the beginning of the set, but not the end, because you don't really know the end; you will include pictures without rewriting the captions; you will cut and paste big chunks of complex material from the original source, because you are not sufficiently familiar with the texts to adapt them and rewrite them for the new situation.

Understanding the materials

In the week between receiving the materials and the exam you have to organise and understand the source materials. Understanding the information means comprehension: making it meaningful to yourself. If you don't understand it, then you'll never be able to retell it to your audience.

How do I make sure I understand?

Understanding the information doesn't always come easily or quickly. Reading it, rereading it and organising the information will help. Other techniques are more basic, such as using a dictionary or thesaurus. One student assumed 'hospice' meant 'hospital', with disastrous results. When asked why she had not looked the word up in a dictionary, she confessed, 'I didn't think of that'. If *you* cannot think why the outcome was so disastrous, go and look up the meaning yourself.

Making a start: adopt a method

There is no set method for preparing the materials, but a suggested (and tried and tested) way of doing it is described below. It suggests that you go through the materials a number of times, each time reading with a different purpose in mind. This means that there is more chance of you reading purposefully and maintaining interest. You are less likely to lock onto the easier texts and ignore the complex material that needs effort to understand. The result will be an answer based on a wide selection of materials and with much rewriting — criteria for success in the higher mark bands.

Adopting a method can help you to read systematically and get a sense of the collection as a whole. Without such an approach it is all too easy to prepare the beginning thoroughly and lose interest before the end. Remember that the materials have been randomly sequenced, so you have no framework to guide you through them unless you supply it.

(1) Tag the articles

Separate out the articles in the pack and number them. Sum up the main content of each text. This process is known as **tagging**.

(2) Catalogue, summarise and gloss

Make a list of the articles, briefly describing the subject, source and date of each piece, to create an inventory (see the sample inventory on p. 34). You need only scan the pieces to do this. You can write the list on the back of the cover sheet. This is **cataloguing** and **summarising**. Then do any necessary **glossing** — look up the meanings of complex words you are unsure of and write them in the margin.

Here are the exam board's rules on preparation, which are reproduced on the pre-release materials:

> The pre-release material taken into the examination may contain brief annotation. Such annotation may include cross-references and/or the glossing of words or phrases. Highlighting and underlining is allowed. Tables of contents, indexes and provisional groupings are permitted. Insertion of pages, loose sheets, 'post-its' or any other form of notes or additional material is not permitted.

So don't think of looking on the internet for a bit more information; that won't help, and will probably hinder.

Students vary enormously in the amount of preparation they do. Some turn up with materials that have received nothing more than a casual flick through. Some turn up with several possible 1,000-word answers written on the sheets. The first group will tend to end up with Es and Us. The second group will be ejected from the exam. The students who achieve As and Bs will be well prepared, but won't have made assumptions about the topic or genre of the task.

(3) Read, discuss or check

Read carefully through each article. You are not allowed to discuss the exam with your teacher(s), but you are at liberty to get together with friends who are sitting the exam. None of you will know which tasks will be set, but you can look at the materials together, which may help you understand any difficult sections. If you are preparing on your own, mark any passages you're still not sure about and come back to them later with a dictionary and thesaurus.

(4) Group your materials

The groups you arrange your materials into should become apparent as you get to know the texts better. Look at your list of articles and look for **themes**. As you do so, you might see two or more ways in which the material could be organised. Make a note of these ways in the margin (see the section 'Planning and finding a structure', p. 37).

Here are examples of sets of materials that have been used in the past, and how they could be grouped:

- **Backpacking** — this set divided into articles that expressed the joys of backpacking and articles that exposed the dangers of backpacking.

- **The Wild West** — this information was split into biographical details about famous figures from the Wild West, such as Calamity Jane and Billy the Kid, and more general historical information.
- **Guinea pigs** — this set divided into information about the housing, feeding and healthcare of guinea pigs, and their different types.

(5) Annotate your materials

Reread the material and intelligently use annotations or a colour-coding method — this is where your judgement and past practice will help. Don't overdo it. If everything ends up highlighted or annotated, the result will be more confusing than enlightening. Overall you are going to reject about 90% of the source material and rewrite about 10% of it. Organisation, practice and system are the keys.

Sample inventory

Below is a sample inventory for the 'Codes and ciphers' materials.

Text	Author	Title	Date	Notes
A	Tom Standage	'Code Breaking and the Dreyfus Affair' in *The Victorian Internet*	1998	
B	Ian Pears	*An Instance of the Fingerpost*	1997	Extract from a novel.
C	Tom Standage	*The Victorian Internet*	1998	Cryptography. Victorian hackers.
D	Tony Sale	*Cipher Systems: the Principle of the Enigma*	2001	Substitution ciphers and the enigma code.
E	Simon Singh	*The Code Book*	1999	Ninth-century code breaking using letter frequencies.
F	Ian Pears	*An Instance of the Fingerpost*	1997	Extract from a novel. Code breaking in the Civil War.
G	Simon Singh	*The Code Book*	1999	The ADFGVX cipher.
H		From internet pages on Beale ciphers		
I	Simon Singh	*The Code Book*	1999	How to crack codes.
J	Robert Harris	*Enigma*	1995	Cracking the enigma ciphers and an extra problem.
K		'The Cryptography FAQ'	1993	Explains basic terms. Early examples — Julius Caesar.
L	Tom Standage	*The Victorian Internet*	1998	Commercial codes used in the nineteenth century.
M		'Speaking in Code', *Independent on Sunday*	6 May 2001	How Comanches developed a special code in the Second World War.

If you skim through this inventory, then already the sources start to take shape:

- *The Code Book* is a major information source, with three extracts.
- Similarly, *The Victorian Internet* supplies three different articles about nineteenth-century code breaking.
- The enigma code is covered in two longer extracts, suggesting it is of major importance.
- The remaining articles are single internet- or newspaper-based pieces.

Recap

Skimming, scanning and reading the materials several times will put you in a strong position long before the exam begins. You should have a good grasp of the information by this time and you will have gone a long way towards organising the materials, so that you can use the sources quickly, efficiently and professionally. You will find that it feels good when you swagger into the exam hall ready for anything.

A word of warning...

You haven't actually written anything yet, but you are now prepared to translate these organised texts into a new coherent whole, without clashes of tone or register.

You may think by now that you know what the task is going to be, so here is a warning: **do not question-spot.** A little mild speculation is as far as you should go. The range of genres you can be asked to reproduce is wide (and getting wider), so trying to guess is pointless.

Decoding the exam question

There are clues in the wording of the exam question that are designed to help you plan and create a successful text. These will identify the context, audience and mode of the piece, and will give hints as to tone and tenor. The purpose of the text will also be apparent, although the task won't state directly 'This should be a persuasive text', for example, as to do so would oversimplify and reduce the potential for different approaches. If you read the question carefully, and take time to think about what is required of you, you should be able to plan your style and approach in an informed and sensible way.

Reading the question carefully can be the key to successful planning. If you simply skim-read the question to get a general idea, pick up your pen and launch into writing, you are likely to miss the subtleties of the requirements of the task.

Example

As an example, read the 'Codes and ciphers' task reproduced on p. 37.

First, the brief identifies the context and genre: an interactive website. This is important, as it identifies where your text will be found (on the internet), the mode (written),

and the medium in which it will exist (on the computer screen). Clearly the word 'interactive' is important too, as it indicates the requirement of the genre that there should be an opportunity for the audience to become involved in some way with the text. This means that you will need to include icons to click on, links to games or questionnaires or a chance for visitors to your website to try encoding or decoding. This is a good opportunity to be creative and use your imagination.

Second, the brief identifies your audience, 'the general public'. This is a wide audience, which brings its own problems and challenges. Your writing will need to be accessible and clear, with any technical lexis suitably glossed and explained, and your sentences should not be too complex. As you are asked to 'introduce' the public to 'the fascinating world of language', you can assume no prior knowledge of any kind.

The purpose of your new text, then, can be taken to be primarily informative, but the word 'fascinating' also implies an interested and lively tone, so you should be careful to avoid a dry, dull catalogue of factual information.

The brief then sets you the task of writing the *'pages* on "Codes and ciphers"' — i.e. pages plural — so you are not required to produce one huge chunk of text, but to organise the material into a number of interlinked pages and sections. The discourse structure of successful web pages tends to be broken up into small chunks of text, which allow easy reading in an on-screen context.

Next the brief requires that you write 'about' 1,000 words. You are not expected to waste time in the exam counting the words on each page and doing a complicated sum at the end of the paper. The examiner's mark scheme states: 'there is no pro rata tariff of mark deduction for infringements of the length requirements'. This will only be a problem if the infringement affects the success of your writing. A text that is hundreds of words over or under the word count is unlikely to work effectively.

To 'Give a brief indication of the layout of the pages', you could draw a plan to show the examiner how your text would look in its finished form. You can label text boxes, and write the text to go in them on the following pages. To illustrate your text you may want to indicate which pictures you would use from the source material pack. You could do this with a simple label, such as 'insert photograph from page 5 here', or alternatively you could actually cut out the picture and glue it into your answer booklet. Taking the glue and scissors approach can make your answer booklet more interesting to look at, but do not lose sight of the fact that this is a language exam.

While you are writing, remember to stop regularly to check how your text is progressing. You will need to make sure you are still on course and following your plan. Whenever there is a natural break in your writing (e.g. at the end of a section), you should read through your work. Check that the materials from different sources are smoothly integrated into your own writing. Proofread to pick up any spelling mistakes or problems with sentence structure. But most importantly of all, remember to ask yourself the question the examiner will ask: 'How effective would this text be for its intended user?'

Writing your draft

Let's assume that you have prepared the pre-release materials thoroughly and that you know the main genres. You have seen a task that you know you can do well, and you have 2 hours 30 minutes in which to write about 1,000 words and a 200-word commentary. You have thought about the audience, the purpose of the writing and the context in which it will be read or listened to. So what is the best way to begin?

Planning and finding a structure

You could just start to write and hope that it all falls out neatly in a conclusion in about 2 hours' time, leaving you 30 minutes in which to write your commentary. But experience shows that this is unlikely to happen. Luckily, there is a better and easier way to write what is required, finish on time and keep control of the writing — by spending just 5 minutes planning.

Think of your 1,000 words as a journey. It is much better to sketch out a route and plan a couple of places where you can pause and change direction. You need a flexible plan that can be adapted as your writing develops.

Below are a task and a rough working plan for the materials on 'Codes and ciphers'.

Task

A new interactive website called *Language Matters* aims to introduce the general public to the fascinating world of language. You have been asked to write the text for the pages on 'Codes and ciphers' using the material provided.
Write about 1,000 words.
Give a brief indication of the layout of the pages.

Plan

- **Introduction** — *Language Matters* website. 'Codes and ciphers' home page. About this web page. Links to main topics. 100 words.
- **First linked page** — what are codes and ciphers? Glossary of terms. 200 words.
- **Second linked page** — 'A Bit of History': how codes and ciphers began. 200 words.
- **Third linked page** — famous codes and ciphers: Beale ciphers, enigma ciphers, ABC code. 200 words.
- **Fourth linked page** — how to write a code. How to crack a code. 300 words.
- Add layout sketches for the home page and a standard page.

Note that a plan would normally include a conclusion, but websites are not linear and so tend not to have an ending as such.

Writing these shorter sections should make the task feel less daunting and more manageable, as well as building a structure into your answer. You can adjust the word length as you write. These factors give you the warm feeling of being in control of your writing, of the time factor in the exam and of the word count. Many examiners are familiar with answers that start well but fade towards the end. Your plan should give your writing a shape and allow you to finish strongly, boosting your marks. Some candidates write well, but end up 200–300 words short of the required length. Planning means you will come in close to target.

Of course, there are many other possible plans. Some candidates took the word 'interactive' in the question to a different level and had sections that allowed viewers to encode and decode messages using different techniques from the sources. This was rewarded in the mark scheme and is a useful example to follow where appropriate, but don't spend too much time planning trivial activities like wordsearches as these will not gain many marks. If you want to include some interactive puzzles, simply create an 'insert' box in your plan.

Writing the commentary

The following extracts from AQA guidance describe the purpose of the commentary and the characteristics of an effective commentary:

> To explain and justify some of the significant decisions [candidates] made whilst planning and constructing their new text and to support their points with a few brief and well-chosen examples…

> The best analysed why certain choices had been made and what effect such choices had upon the text.   (Examiner's report, January 2004)

The commentary is worth 10 of the 70 marks available in Unit 5, and it represents your chance to analyse, evaluate and put into context what you have achieved in your new text and the decisions you took while writing it. Imagine the examiner hovering at your shoulder, asking occasionally, 'Why are you doing it that way?' The sum of your answers is what makes up your commentary.

A limit of 200 words will not allow you to write about everything you have done. You need to discuss and highlight your most important language decisions and show that they were deliberate and thought through.

Strengths

Try to highlight your strengths. If you think you selected the appropriate information for your audience, or that you rewrote and glossed information in a successful manner, then say something about your method of doing so and add an example of what you have done.

It will always be appropriate to demonstrate your understanding of audience and purpose, as these skills are essential to success in the exam, so you could start with these areas. For example:

> The purpose of the programme is to inform and entertain. The audience would be predominantly adult and educated, demanding interesting content as well as anecdote. The fact that it is not an informative lecture means that the register can be less formal.

Sometimes it helps to explain to an examiner what you were trying to do even if you manage it. You might identify something that the examiner had not noticed about the thinking behind your writing:

> I tried to adapt and simplify the spelling rules so that my audience could understand them, but they are so complex I may not have succeeded.

Terminology

By this stage in the course you should be familiar and comfortable with a range of technical terms and the frameworks for analysis should be second nature to you (AO3ii). The frameworks have been designed to make it easier for you to describe language features accurately and with precision. This is preferable to impressionistic and colloquial language. The marking criteria mention 'using appropriate terminology and accurate and coherent written expression' (AO1), and 'understand, discuss and explore concepts and issues' (AO4), so you gain credit for using an appropriate linguistic register. Make sure that you back up your points with examples from your new text.

What to avoid

- **Self-satisfied commentaries.** Finding the task easy and thinking that you have not misjudged anything probably means that you have underestimated it.
- **Purely descriptive accounts of the selection of material and the text created without analysis.** If you find yourself writing 'then I decided to write a bit more about the Millennium Bridge', you are definitely not scoring high marks.
- **Explaining what you could have done but didn't.** Don't make comments such as 'If I had had more time, I would have written layout instructions'. Focus on what you did and why.
- **Pre-planned formulas for commentary writing.** You cannot predict the task, and you shouldn't try to, so you won't know in advance what significant choices will be needed.
- **Repeating or paraphrasing the task set,** using up lots of words without specific reference to your own new text.
- **Mentioning features that are not there.** One student wrote 'I knew the text was to be for a child audience, so I used simple lexis', and yet incorporated words such as 'clandestine' and 'maleficent' without explanation.
- **Generalised feature spotting.** This means identifying something you did (e.g. 'I used a variety of sentence types'), without going on to make a sensible point about what you hoped to achieve by doing so.

Leave yourself enough time to write a commentary. Without doing so you are throwing away 10 marks for something that can be done well in 15 minutes. It is a statement of the obvious, but too many students give cursory attention to this simple task.

Quote yourself

If you rewrote the sources to give a friendlier, less formal tone, then put in a short example to show what you did. If you simplified the lexis, then give a 'before and after' example. Remember: 'A list of linguistic terms without illustration is not illuminating' (Examiner's report, 2003).

Practise, practise, practise

If you have more time than you expected for the commentary at the end of the exam do not be tempted to write too much more than the suggested amount. Although the word limit need not be adhered to slavishly, you should not go on when you have nothing more useful to say. It is helpful to read the chief examiners' reports on the AQA website (**www.aqa.org.uk**). Here is the 2004 section on the commentary:

> These are now established as a further opportunity for candidates to show their awareness of the skills utilised in the text. A fairly average text can be lifted by an analytical approach to the challenges involved, even an awareness that they were not fully met. Despite the constraints of the suggested word limitation, some candidates wrote thoughtfully, with clear supportive evidence from the text. A structured approach considering such aspects as range and context of audience, selection, voice, and constraints of the genre was usually more effective than a shopping list which picked out unrelated language features such as alliteration, metaphor or a set agenda of 'selection, lexis, graphology, syntax, content'. Weak commentaries merely rehearsed the task, summarised the content, focussed on layout and presentation features and threw no light on significant choices. The excessively lengthy 'scatter-gun' approach in which the candidate mentions every aspect of language use and choice they can think of is counter-productive and ultimately self-penalising.

The key to success...

- Prepare the pre-release materials.
- Know the genres and practise writing in them.
- Decode the question.
- Identify and sustain an appropriate tone and style.
- Work to the word limits and time constraints.
- Give yourself time to write the commentary.

Questions
&
Answers

This section looks at examples of students' responses to editorial writing tasks, taken from a real exam situation. It considers these from an examiner's point of view to show you how marks, and ultimately grades, are awarded. This should help you to identify the strengths and weaknesses of your own writing, so that you can develop your exam technique and feel confident that you can produce a text that will impress an examiner.

This part of the guide also considers the principles outlined in the mark scheme for this unit, as well as some of the criteria necessary to reach the top grade bands.

Examiner's comments

Each of the candidate answers is accompanied by examiner's comments preceded by the icon ℯ. Such comments indicate what is creditable in the answers and why a certain grade would be awarded. Pay particular attention to the strengths and weaknesses identified by the examiner, and treat the examiner's comments as useful advice in your preparation for the exam.

Marking criteria

Students often ask how it is possible to mark editorial writing fairly, when there is no 'right and wrong' and there are a number of possible approaches to each task. It is true that this is not a conventional exam paper, and therefore no one can say 'this is the answer'. Rather, the paper demands that you complete a writing task, and this effectively puts the examiner in the role of editor, radio producer, publisher, information officer or publicity agent. So, when marking, the examiner must ask: 'How effective would this text be for its intended user?'

There is no checklist of requirements for each task, so there is no need to try to second-guess what the examiner is looking for. You are free to interpret the task in whatever way makes sense to you, as long as the finished product would work as a successful new text that suits the specified audience, purpose and context.

The marking criteria used by examiners can be broken down into six broad categories. These are given below, along with some of the questions that the examiner will be asking as he/she reads your script.

Text

- Has the candidate constructed a new text?
- Is the new text cohesive?
- Are excerpts from the source material contextualised so that they fit the new text?
- What is the proportion of the source material to the candidate's own writing?
- Has the selected source material been blended effectively with the candidate's own writing?

Tenor

- Is the text written coherently?
- Has it got something to say?
- Is it going somewhere?
- Has the selection of material been guided by a clear idea?
- Has the candidate kept the task clearly in mind throughout the script?
- Does the candidate use argument, narrative, exposition etc., where appropriate?
- Are the sequencing, structure of information and argument, and the movement of ideas clear throughout the text?
- Has the writer understood the purpose of the assignment?

Tone

- Who is the text speaking to?
- Does the text address the audience appropriately?
- Does the candidate show control over his/her use of language?
- Has the source material been glossed/paraphrased/simplified where necessary?

- What communication strategies have been employed?
- Does the text show awareness of the specified audience?
- Does the text use an appropriate voice when addressing the reader/listener?

Genre

- Has the appropriate genre been used?
- Does the writing follow appropriate genre conventions (e.g. introduction, conclusion, subheadings, notes, instructions etc.)?
- Does the candidate show control over the form in which the text is presented?
- Has the writer used an appropriate register and discourse?

Range of source material

- How much of the original source material has the candidate used in the construction of the new text?
- Is it adequately represented (50–65%)?
- Is it comprehensive (over 65%)?

Length

- Has the writer produced a text of the length specified?
- Does any shortfall or excess of words limit the success of the text?

If these questions seem daunting, don't worry — your writing will be marked positively and open-mindedly. The examiner will be looking for evidence that allows him/her to answer 'yes' to these questions. Essentially he/she is looking for a new text that successfully fulfils the requirements set out in the question.

Student answers

The example responses below were written in answering the June 2002 exam paper. The topics are:

- 'Codes and ciphers' — this pack related to the history of enciphering and deciphering messages, as well as explaining some of the technical aspects of codes.
- 'Gateshead Quays' — this pack included information on the history and recent redevelopment of Gateshead, in the northeast of England.

You may need to refer to the pre-release materials from this exam for clarification. You should be able to obtain them through your school or college, by telephoning AQA directly or by visiting the AQA website (www.aqa.org.uk). Even if you cannot get hold of the packs, it is useful to study the examples and the examiner's comments, and to judge how effective the new texts are in relation to the task given. How well do they suit their audience and purpose?

Question 1

Here are two exam responses to the 'Codes and ciphers' question (reproduced on p. 37). The first was written by Charlene, who was awarded 58/60 marks — a grade A. The second answer was written by Dennis, who got 48/60 marks for his response, which is a grade B.

■ ■ ■

A-grade answer

Page 1

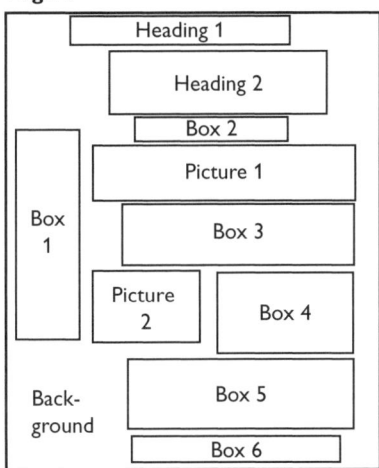

Page 2

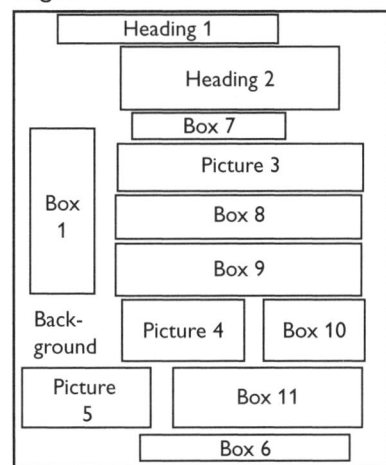

Page 3

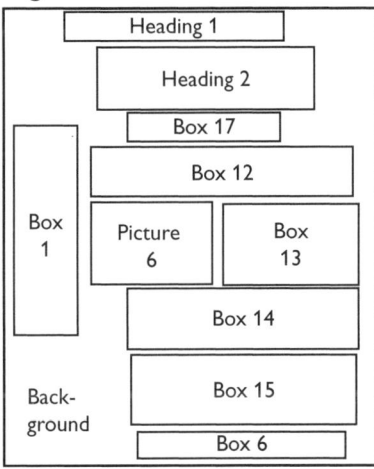

Page 4

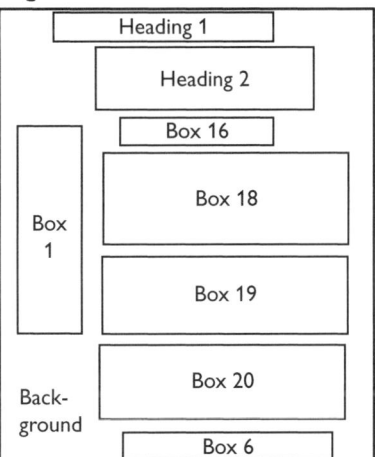

🖉 This is a highly organised approach.

Page 1

Heading 1 | Language Matters | (in bold and also a link back to Language
                                            Matters home page)

Heading 2 | Codes and ciphers | (in fancy font)

Box | Introduction to codes and ciphers | (link to page 1)
(navigation bar)
                  | The Enigma | (link to page 2)

                  | Frequency analysis | (link to page 3)

                  | Code stories | (link to page 4)

Box 2 Introduction to codes and ciphers (in bold font, same size as Heading 1)

Picture 1 | DV DD DD DV FG FD DV DD AV XG AD GX |

Box 3 Did you understand any of that? Probably not, the reason being it is an enciphered message. If you're new to all of this, and have no idea what a cipher is, then here's a list of definitions that will help you understand what you are reading.

Cryptosystem (also known as a cipher system) This is a method of disguising messages so that only certain people can see through the disguise.

Cryptography This is the art of creating and using cryptosystems.

Cryptanalysis This is the art of breaking cryptosystems. It means seeing through the disguise even when you're not supposed to be able to.

🖉 The candidate makes an effective extension of the 'disguise' metaphor.

Cryptology This is the study of cryptography and cryptanalysis.

Plaintext This is what the original message is called.

Cipher text This is what the disguised message is called.

Encryption This means any procedure to convert plaintext into ciphertext.

Decryption The opposite of encryption, this is the procedure to convert ciphertext into plaintext.

Got that? Are you ready to decrypt the ciphertext at the beginning of the page?

Box 4 The ciphertext was created using what is called the 'ADFGVX' cipher.

Encryption begins by drawing up a 6 × 6 grid and filling the 36 squares with a random pattern of 26 letters and 10 digits. Each row and column of the grid is identified by one of the 6 letters, A, D, F, G, V, or X. The arrangement of the numbers and letters in the grid acts as part of the key, so the receiver must know the details of the grid in order to decipher messages.

Picture 2

	A	D	F	G	V	X
A	8	p	3	d	1	n
D	l	t	4	o	a	h
F	7	k	b	c	5	z
G	j	u	6	w	g	m
V	x	s	v	i	r	2
X	9	e	y	0	f	q

So, for example, 8 would be substituted by AA, and P would be replaced by AD.

Now see if you can decrypt the ciphertext at the top. You didn't really think I was going to do it for you, did you?

(Written upside down)
Answer: attack at 10 p.m.

Box 5 Did you know...?
When Julius Caesar sent messages to his acquaintances, he didn't trust the messengers. So he replaced every A by a D, every B by an E and so on through the alphabet. Only someone who knew the 'shift by 3' rule could decipher his messages.

Box 6 ⌐ Back to top of page ⌐ (link to top of page)

Page 2

Box 7 The Enigma (in same style font as Box 2)

Picture 3

```
ABCDEFGHI JKLMNOPQR STUVWXYZ
  ABCDEFGHI JKLMNOPQR STUVWXYZ
```

Box 8 As mentioned briefly on the previous page, Caesar used substitution ciphers, as shown in the image above. Both the recipient and the sender need to know the displacement between the two alphabets, so that they can encipher and decipher messages. But there is one large flaw: there are only 26 messages keys and anyone can just try them out and crack the ciphers.

Box 9 A more sophisticated system uses a random series of characters for the lower alphabet such as:

```
ABCDEFGHI JKLMNOPQR STUVWXYZ
IPHBOSFCQZ JNTWGLMYRXDKEUVA
```

Now the recipient has to know the substitution alphabet. There is a huge number of possible substitutions. If you really must know the exact number, then there are 403,291,461,126,605,635,584,000,000 for an alphabet of 26 letters. Now that's a lot!

But such encipherments are still easily broken by using common-sense facts such as that 'e' is the most common letter, 'the' is the most common word, and so on.

By the twentieth century it became possible to carry out substitutions in rotation, using electrical connections to mechanise the encipherment and decipherment of messages. This is what led to the Enigma machine.

The basic Enigma machine was invented in 1918 by Arthur Scherbius.

Picture 4

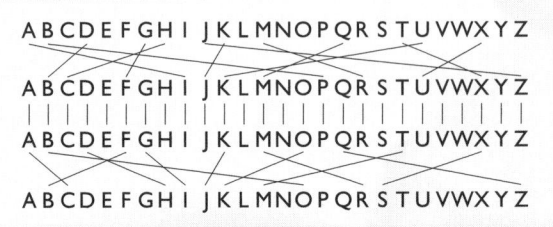

Box 10 Now comes the sciencey bit. The voltage appearing at the G terminal (on the first row) carries on to the F terminal on the middle row, which is then carried over to the B terminal on the bottom row. Wouldn't decrypting a message written on this system be a nightmare?

Mentioning science is an effective cultural reference.

Box 11 Now, that's a little complicated, but imagine using the ancient Caesar shift and displace the second set of wirings by two letters, like this:

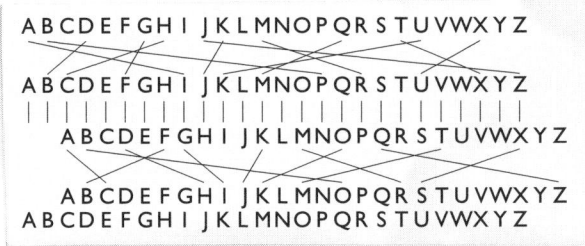

To enable all these shifts and substitutions, the wiring should be on wheels, so the shifts are achieved by rotations of one wheel against another.

Picture 5
the military Enigma machine

TOPFOTO

Page 3

Box 12 Frequency analysis (same style as Box 2)

Box 13 On the previous page, I mentioned the letter 'e' being the most frequently used letter. It was probably Abu Yusuf Ya'qub ibn Is-haq ibn as-Sabbah ibn 'omran ibn Ismail al-Kindi (known as al-Kindi to his friends) who first discovered the technique of exploiting frequencies of letters to break ciphers.

He wrote his 290 books in the ninth century in Arabic, but I shall write his wisdom in English. His technique is called 'frequency analysis'. It is used to decipher messages instead of looking for keys or the shifts in alphabets.

First of all, it is necessary to study a lengthy piece of normal English text to establish the frequency of each letter. Or you could take the easy option and use the picture below.

Picture 6

Letter	Percentage
a	8.2
b	1.5
c	2.8
d	4.3
e	12.7
f	2.2
g	2.0
h	6.1
i	7.0
j	0.2
k	0.8
l	4.0
m	2.4

Letter	Percentage
n	6.7
o	7.5
p	1.9
q	0.1
r	6.0
s	6.3
t	9.1
u	2.8
v	1.0
w	2.4
x	0.2
y	2.0
z	0.1

Box 14 Next, you examine the ciphertext in question. If the most common letter in the text ciphertext is 'j', for example, then it would seem likely that this is a substitute for 'e'. If the second most common letter in the ciphertext is 'p', then this is probably a substitute for 't', and so on.

Box 15 However, it is not possible to apply al-Kindi's recipe for cryptanalysis unconditionally, because the list of frequencies in the table above is only an average and will not correspond exactly to the frequencies of every text.

For example, a brief message such as 'From Zanzibar to Zambia and Zaire, ozone zones make zebras run zany zigzags' shows that short ciphertexts are likely to deviate from the standard frequencies and will be difficult to decipher.

Box 16 Did you know...?
Many industries, such as fishing, mining, banks, railroads and insurance companies have their own codes. For example, Detwiller & Street, a fireworks manufacturer, devised its own code, in which the word 'festival' meant 'a case of three mammoth torpedoes'.

Page 4
Box 17 Code Stories (same style as Box 2)

Box 18 In the nineteenth century, there was a code called the Baravelli code which was created by none other than a man called Baravelli. It became an infamous code when in 1894 a torrent of telegrams were exchanged between the Count of Turin, a nephew of the King of Italy, and the Duchess Graziola, a legendary Italian beauty, staying in Paris.

The head of the French army intelligence thought this had all the hallmarks of a spy communicating with his spymaster, so he ordered the messages to be decoded. But nobody could make head or tail of any of them, because they were all written in numbers. Eventually, a French agent broke into the duchess's rooms and found a small, highly scented book: her Baravelli codebook. The messages were soon decoded and found to express nothing more than 'simple, elementary, natural feeling', a correspondence between lovers, not spies.

Box 19 Tinkering with codes and ciphers was a common hobby among Victorian gentlemen. Wheatstone and Babbage were both keen crackers of codes and ciphers — in effect Victorian hackers.

On one occasion, Wheatstone cracked the cipher used by an Oxford student to communicate with his young lady in London. (In those day, messages appeared in code in newspaper advertisements.)

When the student inserted a message suggesting that they run away together, Wheatstone inserted a message of his own, also in cipher, advising her against it. The young woman inserted a desperate, final message: 'Dear Charlie; write no more. Our cipher is discovered!'

The candidate has selected entertaining anecdotes.

Box 20 Did you know...?
During the Second World War, a handful of Native Americans were used as code-talkers for the Allies. They spoke into walkie-talkies. They were used because their language, Comanche, had never been written down and only a few people could speak it, therefore making it ideal as an 'uncrackable code' to beat the Nazi intelligence services.

Examiner's verdict

This exam response is strong on informative content, which suits the purpose of the task, and draws on a wide range of relevant materials from the source pack. There is clear control and organisation of the information used, demonstrating that the candidate has a coherent idea of where the text is going, and this is clearly signposted for the reader. The voice adopted is suitable for the intended audience.

Strengths

- Exemplary control and organisation of material.
- Sustained clarity and focus on task.

- Cohesive structure — links are made between pages with topics being developed on successive pages.
- The structure is repeated across the four pages, e.g. the 'Did you know...?' sections.
- Awareness of the genre's conventions and practical considerations — page form, navigation bar, links to top of page, text boxes, time to load pages etc.
- The text is arranged into short, accessible chunks, appropriate for the genre.
- Clear headings and signposting make it easy for readers to find their way around the text.
- Strong informative content and excellent coverage of the subject, using a good range of sources.
- The source material is well integrated into a new tone and style — some good rewriting means you cannot 'see the joins'.
- Clear explanation (for the most part) of complicated systems, with integrated use of illustrations from the source pack to aid clarity.
- Illustrations are tied into the body of text and not just 'tagged on'.
- Glossing of terms shows audience awareness.
- Good use of voice, tone and register — not too formal and distant, but not too chatty; it encourages engagement by addressing the audience directly, with personal pronouns and audience-directed questions, and there is good use of humour in places.
- There are entertaining stories relating to codes and ciphers to keep readers interested in the subject.

Weaknesses
- The significance of the Enigma machine is not explained.
- There are some technical flaws.
- The interactive features are not entirely convincing.

Assessment criteria

So how does this verdict match up with the criteria identified in the examiners' mark scheme? According to the scheme for this question, answers in the top band (51–60 marks) must meet the following descriptors:

- The writer is fully aware of, and exploits successfully, the conventions of web pages.
- The text successfully engages the attention of the readers and addresses them in a sustained and appropriate voice; there is a comprehensive range of new writing.
- There is an exemplary selection of material, with all aspects of the task covered.
- There is a structure for the pages that is entirely effective and which is clearly signposted.
- There are suitable illustrations and extracts fully and coherently integrated into the new text, with informative and clear use of captioning etc.
- The writer demonstrates sophisticated writing skills that are sustained to an appropriate length.

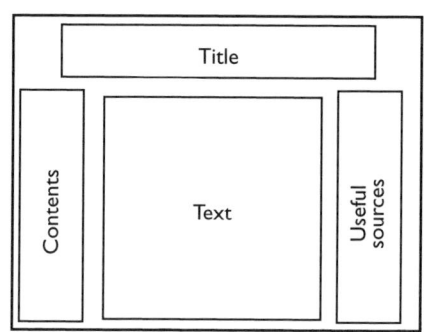 Hopefully you can see how **Charlene** met these criteria and achieved **58/60 marks.** The most heavily weighted assessment objective for this question is **AO2,** which deals with writing for audience and purpose (see the **Introduction** to this guide). **Charlene** shows consistent attention to her audience's requirements and to her intended purpose. She adapts the source material skillfully to create a successful new text.

■ ■ ■

B-grade answer

Plan
'World of Language'
Website — other companies' ads
         — contents list @ one side
            — interactive — questions
                    — answers
                    — exercises etc.

General public — no over-complicated words.

(1) Terms explained
(2) Cryptography — Wheatstone
(3) Development of code systems
(4) Different types of codes/ciphers
(5) Military codebreaking
(6) Enigma

Introduction
Welcome to the world of secret languages, languages which are created for personal use in business, peer groups and in government departments. This section will help you understand the reasoning behind codes and ciphers.

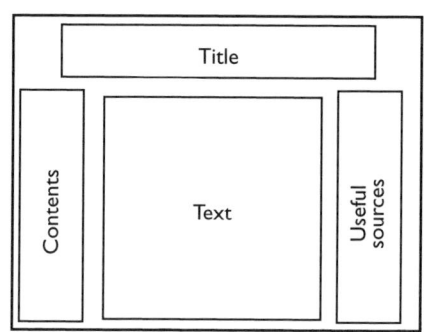 This opening has a friendly, accessible tone and addresses the audience directly.

Before we talk about codes and ciphers here are some useful words which might need explaining.

Cryptosystem or cipher system A method of disguising messages so that only certain people can see through the disguise.

Ciphertext The disguised message.

Cryptography The art of creating and using cryptosystems.

Cryptanalysis The art of breaking cryptosystems, i.e. seeing through the disguise when you're not supposed to be able to.

Cryptology The study of both cryptography and cryptanalysis.

🖉 This clear glossing in everyday language shows audience awareness.

(1) When did cryptology begin?

Starting these sections with questions is a useful way of organising material and orientating the audience. The questions act as cohesive, signposting devices.

It dates back as far as the years of Julius Caesar. He sent messages to his trusted acquaintances, however he didn't trust the messengers. So he replaced every

> **A by a D**
> **B by an E**

and so on.

This became known as the 'shift by 3' rule. People who knew that D represented A, for example, could decipher (solve) his messages. Click here to learn more about the different codes (insert icon).

🖉 Interactive links show confidence with the genre.

Cryptology was a common hobby among Victorian gentlemen. Two keen Victorian code hackers, Wheatstone and Babbage, often enjoyed the task of unscrambling messages that appeared in code in newspaper classified advertisements. These coded messages were a popular way for young lovers to communicate, since a newspaper could be brought into a house without arousing suspicion, unlike a letter or telegram.

On one occasion Wheatstone cracked the code of a seven-page letter written 200 years earlier by Charles I entirely in numbers. Wheatstone also managed to devise a cunning form of encryption known as Playfair's Cipher. Babbage invented several ciphers of his own.

(2) Why did code systems develop?

Many companies chose to develop their own codes for private use with their correspondents overseas, either because:

* they wanted additional security
* existing codes failed to meet the vocabulary needs of those in a specialised field

Code systems developed during the 1870s due to the growth in submarine telegraphy, which meant that messages could be sent to distant lands, at a price of course.

(3) Different codes for different people (linked with 'shift by 3' rule)
The ABC code
This code was compiled by William Clausen-Thue in the 1870s. He was a shipping manager. It was the first commercial code to sell in really large quantities.

The code had a vast vocabulary that represented many common phrases using a single word. This proved to be to an advantage when sending intercontinental telegrams, since they were extremely expensive.

Click here to see an example of a commercial code such as the ABC code (insert icon).

Here is the example of a commercial code.

> FLOUR MARKET FOR COMMON AND FAIR BRANDS OF WESTERN IS LOWER, WITH MODERATE DEMAND FOR HOME MADE AND TRADE EXPORT; SALES, 8000 BUSHELS, GENESSEE AT $5.12. WHEAT, PRIME IN FAIR DEMAND, MARKET FIRM, COMMON DESCRIPTION DULL, WITH A DOWNWARD TENDENCY; SALES, 4000 BUSHELS AT $1.10. CORN, FOREIGN NEWS UNSETTLED THE MARKET; NO SALES OF IMPORTANCE MADE. THE ONLY SALE MADE WAS 2500 BUSHELS AT 67c.

> This could be reduced to: BAD CAME AFT KEEN DARK ACHE LAIN FAULT ADOPT, a mere nine words.

✓ The candidate shows sustained control of the genre and good use of the source material.

(4) Ciphers — complicated or easy peasy?

'A cipher is only a collection of letters on a page,' Iain Pears said in 1997.

In order to decipher a message you need the book on which the code is based. The book will determine the sequence of the cipher.

Cipher systems

The objective is to make it impossible for any interceptor to decrypt the message.

Substitution ciphers (linked with Enigma machine)

These ciphers involve substituting one letter for another according to some rule.

The simplest example of substitution is the Caesar's cipher

> A B C D E F G H I J K L M N O P Q R S T U V W X Y Z
> A B C D E F G H I J K L M N O P Q R S T U V W X Y Z

The letter on the bottom row is written down as the substitution for the text letter on the top row. The received cipher is looked up in the bottom row and the text letter read off from the top row above it.

Confused? Or is it straightforward?

Click to vote

Click to view results of poll 👁

📝 The layout and sequence of the material are clear. The interactive feature shows knowledge of the genre, even if purpose of the vote is unclear.

Enigma machine

The basic Enigma machine was invented by Arthur Scherbius in Berlin in 1918.

Its purpose was to encipher a message by performing a number of substitutions one after the other.

Scherbius's idea was to achieve these substitutions by electrical connections.

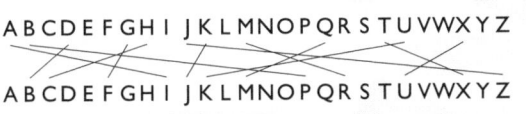

The above diagram shows just a few of the 26 wires that will give the effect of the substitutions, discussed earlier. Click here to go back to substitution ciphers (insert icon).

The way it works

(1) Twenty-six press switches — one for each letter.

(2) A battery is connected to the top letter terminal where the key is pressed.

(3) The voltage flows through the connecting wires to finally light one of a set of lamps, which are connected one to each letter on the bottom row.

For example if 'Q' on the top line is pressed the lamp on the bottom line 'M' will light. Therefore Q → M.

📝 This section shows clear control over and understanding of complex material.

Enigma's rotors

To enable all 26 possibilities to be used, the wiring embodying the substitutions was set in a wheel rather than in strips. The shifts are achieved by rotations of one wheel against another.

The next step was to introduce a third wheel in series, as different relative displacements of the wheels will then give rise to 26 × 26 = 676 different substitution alphabets.

During the Second World War the Enigma machine was used by the Germans and it had a specially adapted fourth rotor, which made it 26 times more difficult to break. Only the U-boats carried it. It was called the Shark, as all German ciphers were named after sea creatures. The Shark Enigmas were the crown jewels of the German Navy.

📝 This section is a little underdeveloped.

Al-Kindi's frequency analysis

To use this technique you must study a lengthy piece of normal English text in order to establish the frequency of each letter of the alphabet, as shown in the table.

Table 1 This table of relative frequencies is based on passages taken from newspapers and novels, and the total sample was 100,362 alphabetical characters. ~~The table was compiled by H. Beker and F. Piper, and originally~~ ~~published in Cipher Systems: The Protection Of Communication.~~

Letter	Percentage	Letter	Percentage
a	8.2	n	6.7
b	1.5	o	7.5
c	2.8	p	1.9
d	4.3	q	0.1
e	12.7	r	6.0
f	2.2	s	6.3
g	2.0	t	9.1
h	6.1	u	2.8
i	7.0	v	1.0
j	0.2	w	2.4
k	0.8	x	0.2
l	4.0	y	2.0
m	2.4	z	0.1

Then examine the ciphertext and work out the frequency of each letter. For example if the most frequent is 'j' then it seems likely that it is substituted for 'e'.

📝 'You must study' is a heavy use of the deontic modal. However, the edited table shows that the candidate is thinking carefully about the material.

The ADFGVX cipher

This cipher features both substitution and transposition.

	A	D	F	G	V	X
A	8	p	3	d	1	n
D	l	t	4	o	a	h
F	7	k	b	c	5	z
G	j	u	6	w	g	m
V	x	s	v	i	r	2
X	9	e	y	0	f	q

Encryption begins by drawing up a 6 × 6 grid and filling the 36 squares with a random arrangement of the 26 letters and 10 digits. Each row and column of the grid acts as part of the key.

(1) Take each letter of the message. Locate its position in the grid and substitute it with the letters that label its row and column.

Message	attack at 10pm										
Plaintext	a	t	t	a	c	k	a	t	1	0	p	m
Stage 1 Ciphertext	DV	DD	DD	DV	FG	FD	DV	DD	AV	XG	AD	GX

(2) The letters of the keyword (MARK shared with receiver) are written in the top row of a fresh grid.

(3) Ciphertext is written underneath it in a series of rows.

(4) The columns of the grid are rearranged so that the letters of the keyword are in alphabetical order.

(5) The final ciphertext is achieved by going down each column and then writing out the letters in this new order.

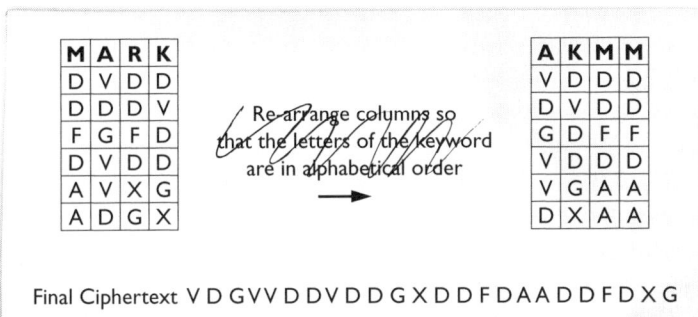

Final Ciphertext V D G V V D D V D D G X D D F D A A D D F D X G

The final ciphertext would be transmitted in Morse Code and the receiver would reverse the encryption process to retrieve the original text.

Military code talkers

It didn't take long for the army to realise just how important code talkers were. During the Second World War Native American soldiers were used to devise codes from their native language. The Comanche language had no words to describe the machinery of modern warfare, so they had to resort to metaphors:

Bomber ⟶ pregnant birds

Automatic weapons ⟶ sewing machines

Hitler/Führer ⟶ crazy white man

🖉 This section shows clear incorporation of the material. The tone is engaging.

This code meant that they could communicate sensitive information with a speed that other encryption methods — such as Enigma code — lacked.

With German soldiers all around it was essential that messages were sent in code. If the enemy realised the details of their plans they might make a final desperate push to overcome them.

The Germans were baffled by the Comanche code. They never found a way of deciphering the messages.

Thank you for visiting this site. I hope you have learnt a lot!

Layout

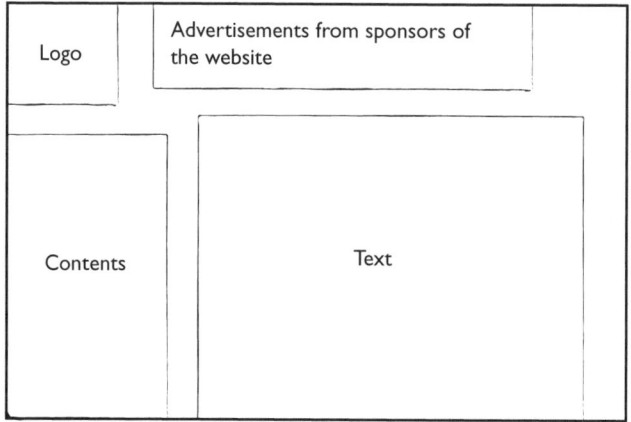

Contents   Introduction
When did cryptology begin?
Why did code systems develop?
Different codes for different people
Ciphers — complicated or easy?
Military code talkers

The layout has to be clear with the links clearly marked out. Having the contents listed at the side means that readers can click on what they are interested in.

📝 This attention to the layout demonstrates genre awareness and provides evidence of planning and organisation of the material.

Examiner's verdict

📝 Dennis's answer displays the following strengths and weaknesses.

Strengths

- Web-page format achieved clearly.
- Range, depth and clear organisation.
- Recognises and engages with the interactive nature of the genre and context, showing awareness of the generic conventions.
- Retains control over material and genre.
- Clear and coherent rewriting of material.
- Well selected and clearly organised use of the source material.
- Comprehensive range of informative content covered.
- Provides a clear introduction to the topic.
- Explanation aimed at a general public audience is sustained throughout.
- Discourse structure appropriate for genre.
- Good use of illustrative material.
- Good audience awareness shown through glossing and reworking.

Weaknesses

- Tone lacking in vitality and is inconsistent.
- Too long, particularly towards the end.
- The answer loses force and tails off.

Assessment criteria

So how does this verdict compare with the examiner's mark scheme? The criteria for band 2 (41–50 marks) are as follows:

- Makes effective use of the conventions of web pages.
- Engages the attention of readers and addresses them in an appropriate voice; a range of new writing.
- Good selection of material with all aspects of the task covered.
- Creates an effective structure for the pages, which is usually clearly signposted.
- Suitable illustrations and extracts incorporated into the new text in a coherent way and to advantage, with effective captioning etc.
- Writes fluently and at appropriate length; sustained writing skills.

Dennis clearly achieves the standard necessary to meet these criteria, but he lacks the sustained focus and tone to move into the higher band. The examiner has awarded him a mark towards the top end of the 41–50 mark band in recognition of how well he has selected material from the source pack and adapted it for the appropriate genre, purpose and audience. You should be able to see how he earned 48/60 for this response.

■ ■ ■

Question 2

Here is the audio task for the 'Gateshead Quays' source material. This kind of task requires that you write a text to be spoken aloud, so mode plays an important part in constructing a new text.

The regeneration of Gateshead Quays has been completed and the Visitors' Centre has designed a self-guided walking tour for adults. Visitors can hire an audiotape to listen to as they walk from the Visitors' Centre to the Baltic Centre and the Music Centre.

The tape should describe what has been achieved in the regeneration and should also pay some attention to the history of the quayside and adjoining area. It should engage and entertain the visitor. You do not need to include tour directions.

Write the script for the tape. Use about 1,000 words.

Your text should be accompanied by a commentary in which you explain some of the significant decisions and choices you have made in writing it. The commentary should be approximately 150–200 words.

Below are two answers to this task. The first was written by Erica. Her answer is strong and she gained 57/60 marks — a grade A. As you read her response, try to think about how the examiner awards marks. It might help if you look back to the beginning of this section to remind yourself of the criteria that the examiner is looking for.

The second response is by Jane. She achieved 38/60 marks (a grade C). There are still many good qualities to her writing, but see if you can spot where she lost marks.

■ ■ ■

A-grade answer

Plan
Format = talk
Audience = adults
Register = formal, but welcoming
Purpose = informative, interesting
Tone = formal, casual
No illustrations. Not too much detail. Sound effects, vary voices.
Include Baltic Centre, Music Centre (not bridge). Mention other features of the scheme.

(Short musical introduction. Fade out.)

(Female voice in no dialect or accent) Gateshead Quays — a place of leisure, pleasure and life-enhancing experiences.

(Short musical break, followed by same voice) The East Gateshead Regeneration Committee welcomes you today to Gateshead Quays and invites you to explore this exciting part of the northeast and see for yourself why it has developed a reputation for leisure, pleasure and life-enhancing experiences.

📝 The music at the beginning shows awareness of the genre and the introduction sets the content that follows.

(Male voice) We're sure that you, like so many before you, will find this area a unique mix of history and modernisation. Should you require further assistance, staff at the Visitors' Centre just left (St Mary's Church), will be more than happy to help you.

📝 The candidate balances the old and the new ('mix of history and modernisation'), while the change to a male voice gives variety. The tone is helpful and friendly.

(Back to female voice) For us to be able to appreciate the amazing landscape that appears before you today, it is important to realise that Gateshead's history has shaped the Quays to its glory now.

📝 The candidate has taken a chronological approach.

(Male voice) So, we'll start at one of the best-known landmarks in Tyneside; St Mary's Church.

(Pause)

(Music — sound of church bells ringing. Fade out.)

(Male voice) St Mary's Church has been a central part of Gatesheaed and its large religious settlement, and, despite being the subject of two fires, this twelfth-century church remains in all its beauty as a reminder of the steep history that surrounds this area.

(Female voice) Throughout its existence, the church has served many purposes, ranging from housing government troops in 1644 to holding auctions, after it became the auction house for Phillips Auctioneers.

This section is succinctly written.

(Male voice) And today, as you've seen, it is still an essential part of the Gateshead Quays' community, existing as the Visitors' Centre.

The candidate makes good lexical choices here.

(Musical break — 30 seconds)

This musical break seems too long.

(Female voice) As you can see around you, the Gateshead Quays are stunning and impressive today. And, just like today, in their former heyday in the nineteenth century the Quays were admired for their prosperity and ability to attract a wide variety of industry.

The candidate makes a good link between past and present.

(Introduce sound effects of cranes, men working — shouts, digging, i.e. sounding 'industrial'. Fade out.)

These are pertinent sound effects.

Gateshead and neighbouring areas such as Pipewellgate prospered in the nineteenth century due to their location, which meant they benefited from access to and from all points of the compass.

(Male voice) This growth continued in the twentieth century, with a huge variety of industry locating there. A worker in one of the factories in the 1930s recalls the area:

(Worker with Geordie accent) All around were factories; chemical works, rope works, cement factories, bread factories, you name it us up here had the lot!

The candidate maintains the chronological approach. The selected excerpts from the source material are incorporated effectively.

(Female voice) But, unfortunately, Gateshead was to suffer from being neighbours with Newcastle. As Newcastle dominated the river trade, Gateshead fell into decline.

This links smoothly with the previous section.

(Sound of industrial doors banging close in background)

(Male voice) Industries closed, and the dense housing that had been built up in areas such as Hillgate, Bottle Street and Pipewellgate were all pulled down as apart of the slum clearance programme of the 1930s. Indeed, the housing was in dire condition, lacking basic local amenities. Betty Davis remembers this vividly:

(Sounds of kids playing. Fade out.)

(Old female voice with Geordie accent) We used to live in Bowl Alley Bank, leading to Pipewellgate. You know, I'll never forget the narrow streets and the cramped houses we played and lived in — but it was home.

(Male voice) And so a once teeming area was cleared and left lifeless.

📝 Betty Davis's recollections are well introduced and contextualised. The candidate uses short sections.

(Musical break — 30 seconds)

(Female voice) But Gateshead was always dynamic. Even after falling into sad decay as the twentieth century marched on, it has reincarnated itself once more as a focal point of the northeast. And you only have to look around to see what a spectacular reincarnation the Quays has had.

📝 This is an effective link to the present day.

(Musical break)

(Female voice) Without forgetting its heritage, Gateshead is booming once again, with one of yesteryear's landmarks proving to be a key piece in the jigsaw that makes up the modern Quays.

(Sound effects of men and women working, production line words etc.)

(Male voice, slow) The Baltic Art Centre — where old and new combine in a breath-taking mix.

(Male voice) Built in 1950 for Joseph Rank, the Baltic was a dual-purpose factory for the production of flour and animal feed. But a fire saw the decline of the factory.

📝 The candidate explains the historical context.

(Female voice) The only remaining part of the factory is the silo building, which you can see now. And it is here that one of the centrepieces of the major arts and leisure quarter will be housed — the Baltic Centre for Contemporary Art. Architect Dominic Williams has redesigned and transformed the old factory, into:

(Different male voice, old) A leading international contemporary visual arts space, set to be one of the largest in Europe.

(Pause)

(Male voice) The stunning Baltic Centre is specifically designed to meet the needs of artists and audiences alike.

Just a few of the things it has to offer include:

(Female voice) Five different galleries.

(Male voice) Cinema and lecture space.

(Female voice) Media lab with the latest technology.

(Male voice) Rooftop restaurants.

To prevent this from being list-like the candidate varies the voices.

With a whole plethora of art to choose from, from painting to new media, art here will always be exciting, always changing and challenging. It's up to you to go and discover all that this ambitious project has to offer.

(Musical break — 30 seconds)

(Male voice, dominant) An icon for the northern hemisphere.

(Pause)

(Female voice) That's what the development agency of the Music Centre at Gateshead wants this spectacular project to be.

The signposting between the previous point and this one is well done.

(Pause, then introduce music — wide variety to show wide variety of music at the centre)

One look at the music centre and you can see that their aim may well be fulfilled.

(Male voice) A visionary centre for the celebration, performance and enjoyment of music for everyone, the Music Centre complements the regeneration programme of Gateshead Quays magnificently. Its make up is simply three buildings under one roof. But what it has to offer, as you will see, is breathtaking.

(Female voice) A 1,650-seat concert hall.

(Male voice) A rehearsal hall.

(Female voice) A home for the Northern Sinfonia and Folkworks.

(Male voice) A music information source.

(Female voice) And much more.

(Male voice) This innovative piece of architecture is already attracting huge interest from around the world, and together with the Baltic Centre and features such as the Millennium Eye Bridge, it means Gateshead is booming: the inflow of jobs and tourism has given a huge boost to the community. And they've all strengthened Gateshead's joint bid for European Capital of culture in 2008.

📝 This looks to the future and shows evidence of 'shaped' text.

(Music)

(Female voice) The huge regeneration programme has certainly helped put Gateshead on the map again. What has been achieved is quite remarkable: it is hard to imagine that the slums and derelict land of Bothe Street have developed into the breathtaking and unique area that surrounds you now.

📝 This locates the listener and demonstrates audience awareness.

(Music builds up as paragraph ends. Then fade out.)

(Male voice) We hope that you've gained a valuable insight into Gateshead Quays and that your visit here is a spectacular as the buildings and history that surround you. The Visitors' Centre has leaflets and brochures with further information.

📝 This section provides good closure to the text.

(Music)

(Male voice saying 'small print' in serious tone) The East Gateshead Regeneration Programme thanks its sponsors and backers in the production of this tape and the entire programme.

Examiner's verdict

📝 This response shows a writer keenly engaged with the task. Erica's tone is light and friendly, but informed and serious, which is a tricky balance to pull off. The new text is well structured and presented as a script, drawing on a wide range of sources.

Strengths
- Clear, assured and well written.
- Always conscious of audience and purpose.
- Strong awareness of context — historically, spatially and architecturally.
- Uses a variety of appropriate and convincing voices to maintain interest, including twin anchors and guest voices.
- Blends the historical and the contemporary smoothly, making historical detail relevant to a modern audience.
- Gives broadly even coverage to the Visitors' Centre, Baltic Centre and the Music Centre.
- Comfortable with the sources and information.
- Strong, cohesive links — both anaphoric and cataphoric.
- Use of appropriate sound effects.
- Well introduced and contextualised for an audience with no prior knowledge.

Weaknesses
- The notion of 'no dialect or accent' is flawed.

Assessment criteria

For this question, the mark scheme identifies the following descriptors as criteria for the top band (51–60 marks):

- Achieves a sophisticated blend and effective balance between the old and the new.
- Conveys information in imaginative ways which sustain interest.
- Maintains an assured, entirely appropriate and convincing speaking voice throughout.
- Shows sophisticated writing skills.

You should be able to see how Erica met these criteria and achieved 57/60 marks. She shows consistent attention to her audience's requirements and her intended purpose, as required by AO2.

■ ■ ■

C-grade answer

Plan

- Short introduction, general information about area and places to visit.
- Regeneration (with achievements).
- Visitors' Centre, St Mary's as focus of area. Historical perspective = Great Fire of Gateshead.
- Mention perambulations.
- Baltic Centre, new use, historical perspective as mill.
- Music Centre, not open yet but assume completed.
- Summary of achievement.
- Offer further attractions of Gateshead people may wish to visit.

Audience: adults
Purpose: inform and entertain
Format: script
Tone: lively

Sound effects, voices.

This plan shows that the candidate has thought about the task requirements.

Northern brass band to indicate beginning

Voice 1 (slight Geordie accent): Newcastle Gateshead Buzzin'. This new slogan perfectly reflects the success of the regeneration on Gateshead Quays. We hope that as you stroll around the area you will experience the unique and welcoming Gateshead way of life. So join us as we step through the 'Gateway to Gateshead'.

This is striking opening, and the music at the start demonstrates attention to mode and medium. The candidate adopts a pleasant tone and uses signposting.

Sound of rushing wind and then a bustling city — visitors will really feel as if they have stepped into something

🖉 These sound effects demonstrate confidence with the genre.

Voice 2: Gateshead has not always had it so good and the life of the former St Mary's Church, now the Visitors' Centre which you have just left, perfectly illustrates this, as does the Baltic Centre, which is also on our whistle-stop tour.

🖉 This shows awareness of the context. The candidate varies the voices to sustain interest.

Voice 1: The first mention of St Mary's was way back in 1291 and since then it has had a strategic part to play in the history of Gateshead, as historian John Blakeley explains…

🖉 This sets up an effective link to John Blakeley's comments.

John Blakeley: St Mary's and its anchorage boast a colourful past. In 1644 government troops were housed there during the English Civil War and then in 1693 it housed the borough's first school. So as you can see it's quite a versatile church.

🖉 This direct address is appropriate to the audience.

Sound of fire quietly crackling

John Blakeley: The most significant part of St Mary's history and Gateshead was the Great Fire of Gateshead when in 1854 a huge explosion and subsequent fire devastated the area. The fire had started in a factory at Hillgate which stored vast quantities of explosive material.

🖉 The candidate makes a historical reference.

Loud bangs of explosion

🖉 The sound effects show consistent attention to the medium and genre.

Voice 2: The fire had a huge impact on the area but St Mary's Church came off quite well. Although seriously damaged, it was lovingly restored by the loyal congregation, with the fine stained glass windows and new tower which you can still see today.

Voice 1: Yet another fire in 1979 marked the end of the church's life as a place of worship. But not one to give up, demonstrating its versatility, the church became an auction house during the last 10 years of the twentieth century.

Voice 2: St Mary's Church still plays a focal role in Gateshead and now acts as the Visitors' Centre, bringing together the regeneration programme.

Voice 1: So if we continue our perambulations as they were called in the eighteenth century — a walk to you or me! — we should end up at the Baltic Centre for Contemporary Art.

🖉 The humorous tone shows an attempt to relate to the audience.

Voice 2: The Baltic Centre is quite literally state of the art and is a key piece of the regeneration jigsaw.

Voice 1: At a towering 42 metres high the Baltic is grand in stature and personality, and like St Mary's it has had a varied past. The site was occupied until 1858 by the Gateshead iron works and lay derelict until the 1950s when the Baltic Flour Mill, built for Joseph Rank, came into use.

Voice 2: So if you take a look at the Baltic be careful not to step too far back into the Tyne! It's behind you!

The candidate is conscious of the context, and the humour sustains the pleasant tone.

Voice 1: Dominic Williams was responsible for the transformation of the Baltic and he explains…

Dominic Williams: The aim was to create an internationally renowned centre for contemporary art — one of the biggest temporary art spaces in Europe.

There is a variety of voices and good use of the source material.

Voice 2: The landmark building has been specifically designed with the art, artists and audience in mind. Some of the features on offer include: five galleries, three artist's studios, a cinema space and a rooftop restaurant to name but a few.

Voice 1: Director of the Baltic Centre, Sune Nordgren, said the Baltic is…

Sune Nordgren: A place where exciting things are created, where nothing is impossible.

Voice 2: Why not visit and see for yourself?

Music of Symphony Orchestra

Voice 1: Yes, you've guessed it. Our next port of call is the stunning Gateshead Music Centre. Prepare to be amazed.

Voice 2: So what's the verdict?

The conversational tone is not quite appropriate.

Voice 1: I think the people of Gateshead are quite rightly proud of their music centre. It had been dubbed one of the most eye-catching buildings in the country — even the world. It was designed to be an icon for the northern hemisphere and what better place for it than Gateshead.

Voice 2: The Music Centre was designed to be a sort of glue bonding the community of Gateshead and it seems to be fairly good glue.

The voices are too interactional and the tone is a little too enthusiastic.

Voice 1: The Music Centre complements the regeneration of the Quays and is a key partner in the region.

Voice 2: It's amazing what can be achieved with a bit of team work. Take a listen…

Symphony Orchestra

Using music here is a good touch.

Voice 1: That was the sound of the Northern Sinfonia, whose home ground is the Music Centre.

Voice 2: Why not take a look around the centre. Gateshead's doors are always open to new friends.

Voice 1: Even without a performance the architecture and sheer atmosphere of the place can keep you entertained for hours.

Voice 2: Well, I'm afraid the Gateshead experience is nearly complete. Although that's not necessarily true. There's so much more to Gateshead than we've had a chance to show you today. Please feel free to ask at the Visitor Centre on your return for further information about some of the attractions on offer at Gateshead.

The candidate is beginning to signpost the conclusion.

Voice 1: Today's Gateshead Quays bears evidence of the layers of history which have seen the river banks change from rural manor land to industrial heartland, falling into sad decay as the twentieth century marched on.

The syntax is too complex for the spoken mode.

Voice 2: But now, as the regeneration programme has reached completion, the river-side is coming to life again in a third guise — as a place of leisure, pleasure and life-enhancing experiences.

This is good use of slogans from the materials.

Voice 1: History, as Gateshead demonstrates, never stands still — around Gateshead's corners there's always something new!

Voice 2: So there we have it — Gateshead in a nutshell. But just before we leave here's a reminder of just some of the other attractions on offer in Gateshead...

Voice 1: The Gateshead Millennium Bridge, Grainger Town, Pipewellgate, Newcastle Barracks and of course, as the Eiffel Tower is to Paris, our very own Tyne Bridge. No visit to Gateshead would be complete without this.

Voice 2: In addition to these attractions look out for the special activities provided as part of Gateshead's joint bid with Newcastle to be UK Capital of Culture in 2008. Ask at the Visitors' Centre for further details.

Voice 1: We hope you have enjoyed our perambulations around Gateshead today and will visit us again soon. Have a safe journey home and don't forget...

Voices 1 and 2: Newcastle Gateshead Buzzin'.

This is a good conclusion with an appropriate tone.

Examiner's verdict

Jane has approached the task confidently, producing a script that makes convincing use of the medium and genre and incorporating excerpts from the source material in a range of voices. She has adopted a good tone and addresses the audience effectively.

However, the script is limited by a number of factors. Jane has written using two main voices, which can be a successful way of breaking up an audio script. However, the two voices are not clearly differentiated, and in places they slip into a tone and style that are too conversational, becoming almost like adjacency pairs. It becomes confusing whether or not they are speaking to the audience. Take a look at this example:

Voice 2: So what's the verdict?

Voice 1: I think the people of Gateshead are...

Is Voice 2 addressing Voice 1, the listener, or both?

But the main flaw in this response is that it is too thin. For a task that has a main purpose of informing listeners about the Gateshead Quays area, there is little substantial information in this script, especially given the wealth of data available in the source pack. In places the tone is too enthusiastic, which, coupled with the lack of detailed information, leads to the script appearing to be a persuasive text. Visitors might be left feeling that they had learned little from the tape.

Strengths
- Good range of rewriting.
- Balance between the old and the new.
- Appropriate use of tone.
- Confident, imaginative use of the medium and approach to genre.
- Well structured and signposted.
- Good use of slogans and some source material.
- Clear thinking about audience and purpose.

Weaknesses
- Not enough substance in the informative content for the purpose.
- Does not use a broad enough range of source material.
- The alternating voices are not differentiated.
- The conversational tone is at the expense of purpose.

Assessment criteria

The mark scheme identifies the following descriptors as criteria for answers to get into the 31–40 mark band for this question:

- Achieves a generally effective blend and balance between the old and the new.
- Conveys information in ways which mostly sustain interest.
- Maintains a generally appropriate and convincing speaking voice throughout.
- Shows fluent and usually effective writing skills.

🖉 **Jane achieved 38/60 marks, which is near the top end of the 31–40 band. This reflects the strengths of this script and its flaws as a piece of writing with an informative purpose.**

Commentaries

Charlene's commentary

I chose a light, lively tenor, and a personal narrative in the text, occasionally using direct speech to the reader, such as 'Understand what you're reading?' This is so the reader can settle down and enjoy the informality which adds a sparkle to the subject of codes and ciphers (and can be understood by both adults and children alike), whereas a prim, formal tone would discourage the reader from clicking on any links and reading further. I also included light, friendly jokes, and created a cohesive structure between the four pages by making comments which I expanded on the following page.

Each page was self-contained, with its own topic and heading, which was included on the navigation bar on the left to enable the reader easy access to and from pages (and also a link back to the Language Matters home page). I split the text up into boxes and did not use too many pictures on one page to allow for easy loading of a page on the reader's screen (also the reason for using four smaller pictures rather than one long, tedious and long-loading page which infuriates internet surfers).

I also included a 'Did you know...?' section on some pages to create a lively, trivial, amusing addition to the web pages, which I personally enjoyed creating.

Examiner's verdict

🖉 Charlene's commentary demonstrates the following strengths:

- Awareness of tone, register and style in response to the task and their effects, although there is some confusion over the technical terminology.
- Reference to specific techniques used to create tone and register.
- Use of detailed supporting examples.
- Awareness of audience and genre.
- Confidence in the use of discourse structure and its effect on the audience.
- Awareness of issues of reader orientation and page navigation.
- Good overview of the structure and cohesion of the text as a whole.
- Keeps sight of the context.

🖉 **Charlene demonstrates a clear overall conception of what the task involves and her own strategy for dealing with it. She has a confident awareness of the genre requirements and discusses the specific problems of writing for web pages. Her** commentary refers to details of the new text, and she identifies the effects these have on the audience. She received 10/10 marks.

This is an example of how an answer does not have to be perfect to achieve full marks. There are some technical inaccuracies in Charlene's writing and she has not addressed how she selected material from the resource packs.

Dennis's commentary

The website was for the general public and it was important to limit the amount of technical language. That is why I included definitions to words that would be unfamiliar in the introduction. The tone of this website has to avoid being too formal because it might have put people off reading it.

The order of the text was important but not a major concern because it was divided into separate sections and there were opportunities for the reader to click on linked sections.

Websites have to be interactive. With that in mind I thought it would be a good idea to include a voting poll where readers can communicate their feelings to the producers of the website. This would be a good form of customer feedback.

Examiner's verdict

Dennis's commentary includes the following strengths and weaknesses:

- Identifies the audience.
- Shows awareness of the specific demands of adapting complex material for the audience.
- Explains a sensible strategy for dealing with these demands and for addressing the interactive nature of the task.
- Identifies the register, but without a specific link to the text or to language features.
- Addresses discourse structure, but vaguely.
- Implies awareness of the genre requirements, but this is not explicitly developed.

Dennis identifies a number of significant factors that had an effect on his new text. He deals specifically with genre and discourse structure, as well as one or two issues relating to audience requirements. However, his commentary suffers from a general lack of development. To improve his grade he needs to develop each point he makes, discussing the style and approach that he used to adapt the source material for the audience and purpose. This involves a more detailed discussion of language features. He needs to explain not only what was done, but exactly how he did it. His commentary would receive 4/10 marks.

Erica's commentary

I thought that since the audience for this talk were adults, the choice of lexis could be sophisticated, e.g. 'contemporary' and 'icon', and sentences could be fairly long and complex and would still be understood.

I decided to have a fairly formal tone, using no slang or colloquialisms, but to keep it inviting, so I opened with 'Welcome' and used personal pronouns such as 'you' and 'us' to create a friendly tenor (and also elision, e.g. 'we're').

To avoid confusion, I decided to have all my historical information at the start of the tape and then progress chronologically to the modern era. But because I linked the two, e.g. 'the slums and derelict land of Bothe Street have developed into...the area that surrounds you now', the listener is constantly reminded of the prior heritage, which I felt was an important feature.

Because the tape was a guide, I made several references such as 'Look around you' and 'which you can see' so that it sounds like a tape heard while there. I also decided to be quite 'promotional' using positive adjectives, as I assumed the writers would want to portray a good image.

Because the only visual stimulus was the surroundings, I had to make the audio exciting and variable. Thus I used two speakers, and included quotes, with regional dialects for authenticity. Music was also used to break up sections and so prevent heavy blocks of writing.

The voices of the main speakers had no dialect or accent. They were therefore accessible to all listeners, even foreigners.

Examiner's verdict

Erica's commentary demonstrates that she is:

- Aware of language choices and effects.
- Able to identify, in detail, a range of language features used to create tone.
- Able to identify specific lexis that suits an adult audience.
- Aware of grammatical choices in response to an audience.
- Able to justify her structural choices.
- Aware of context, giving several examples of strategies to deal with contextual factors.
- Aware of structural and dialect choices, in response to the demands of contextual factors.
- Aware of the genre — for example, mentioning the importance of music to break up the dialogue.

This is a strong commentary. It is full and detailed, and explores Erica's significant choices and decisions in the creation of her new text. She shows the effects that contextual factors and the requirements of audience and purpose had on the style and structure of her writing. She has selected some appropriate examples to support her discussion, and demonstrated a good technical understanding. However, a couple of examples of 'positive adjectives' would have been helpful, and the idea of 'no dialect or accent' is incorrect. Erica received 10/10 marks.

Jane's commentary

Throughout the script I used a number of voices and introduced various different people, such as Dominic Williams, because a variety of voices helps keep the audience's interest and seems more lively. The people I introduced are authorities in their field. The use of sound effects, as well as serving as markers to different sections of the tape, also added to the entertainment value. The voices of the presenters are Geordie, which adds authenticity and makes them seem friendly. I used quite a chatty tone and personal pronouns to engage the listener. I used a number of rhetorical questions to serve as a monitoring device but also they involve the listener.

The sections of text spoken by each voice are quite short as long texts would only bore the listener. When describing the various features I tried to include those which I think the audience would find of interest and not bombard them with facts and figures. I used some humour, e.g. 'perambulations', to add to the entertainment factor. I repeated the slogan 'Newcastle Gateshead Buzzin' at the beginning and end as the audience would remember this.

Examiner's verdict

Jane's commentary includes the following strengths and weaknesses:

- Awareness of audience and tone, and a description of her strategy for dealing with these.
- Awareness of sound effects and discourse structure.
- Identifies 'entertainment value', but does not relate this to the requirements of the task.
- Addresses the effects of dialect and pronouns.
- Mentions monitoring devices, but these are not appropriate to this genre.
- Deals with how she selected the material, though this section is vague and needs development.
- Does not develop the point about using authorities or explain how it is appropriate to the task.

Jane's commentary seems comprehensive at first glance — she has covered many appropriate issues relating to how she constructed her new text, and listed all the key features of her writing soundly and sensibly. But although she has related her points to audience and purpose, she has done so in a perfunctory way, without discussing the demands of the task. In other words she has described what she has done, without fully explaining why she has done it. She received 6/10 marks.

Unit 5 past questions

Listed below is an archive of past Unit 5 exam questions. Past papers and their mark schemes are available from the AQA publications department and on the AQA website.

Exam series	Topic	Task	Genre	Audience
January 2002	(1) Family history	(1) Text for a wall display	(1) Local library wall display	(1) Adult
	(2) Family history	(2) Text for a 'how to…' article	(2) Broadsheet newspaper article	(2) Broad appeal
	(3) Soap	(3) Biography	(3) Biography for an educational resource pack	(3) 11–12-year-olds
	(4) Soap	(4) Script for a dramatised documentary	(4) Radio 4 script	(4) Adult listeners
June 2002	(1) Codes	(1) Text for a feature, 'The secret world of codes'	(1) Broadsheet newspaper's illustrated supplement for young people	(1) 10–15-year-olds
	(2) Codes	(2) Text for 'Language matters' website	(2) Web pages for an interactive website	(2) General public
	(3) Gateshead Quays	(3) Article on the regeneration of the quays	(3) Article for a national rail magazine	(3) General public/rail passengers
	(4) Gateshead Quays	(4) Audio tape describing completed regeneration etc.	(4) Audio tape for a self-guided tour	(4) Visitors to the quays
January 2003	(1) Alternative medicine	(1) Article on alternative medicine including comments and views	(1) Tabloid newspaper article	(1) General public
	(2) Alternative medicine	(2) Leaflet for prospective patients	(2) Information leaflet for a group of practitioners	(2) Prospective patients
	(3) Mountain biking	(3) Script for a programme on mountain biking	(3) Radio 5 script	(3) Mainly adult
	(4) Mountain biking	(4) Web pages entitled 'Mountain biking: your fun ride to fitness'	(4) Website for a local leisure centre	(4) Families
June 2003	(1) Psycho	(1) Radio Times article	(1) Informative article	(1) Adult
	(2) Psycho	(2) Radio 4 programme	(2) Documentary	(2) Radio 4 audience
	(3) Money	(3) Royal Mint leaflet to inform and entertain	(3) Promotional leaflet	(3) Visitors to the Royal Mint
	(4) Money	(4) Wall charts	(4) Information wall chart	(4) 14–16-year-olds

Exam series	Topic	Task	Genre	Audience
January 2004	(1) The Greeks	(1) 2 × 500-word pieces that inform and entertain	(1) Tabloid-style Greek Gazette pages	(1) 9–13-year-olds
	(2) The Greeks	(2) Audio tape on the background of the Olympics	(2) Audio tape for tourists	(2) Adult tourists
	(3) Forgery	(3) Magazine article	(3) Informative article	(3) Adult readership
	(4) Forgery	(4) Radio 4 script	(4) Radio script	(4) Adult audience
June 2004	(1) Glastonbury	(1) Background information for CD inlay	(1) Illustrated booklet	(1) Music lovers
	(2) Glastonbury	(2) Radio documentary	(2) Radio script	(2) Radio 1 listeners
	(3) Spelling	(3) Two posters	(3) Information poster	(3) Key Stage 3 students
	(4) Spelling	(4) Magazine article	(4) Informative article	(4) Parents

Editorial writing to January 2006

Tasks		
Alternative medicine	Gateshead Quays	Music hall
Ancient Greece	Glastonbury	Noah's Ark
Backpacking	Grace Darling	Nurseries
Baseball	Grammar	Panama Canal
Bessie Smith	Grasmere	Pop music
Birds	Guinea pigs	Pressure groups
Black slavery	Ibiza	Psycho
Brass bands	Industrial archaeology	Psycholinguistics
British bridges	Jewish festivals	Raymond Chandler
Calligraphy	Language	Rodin
Castles	Lead mining	Schools
Codes and ciphers	Leeds trams	Second World War servicemen in training
Cuerden Park Nature Reserve	Libyan embassy siege	
Data processing	Management training	Sellafield
Early days of recorded sound	Mars	Soap/Lord Leverhulme
Edward Elgar	The Mary Rose	Spelling
Elizabethan theatre	Miners' Art	Study skills
Emigration to the USA	Minority languages	Tiananmen Square
Family history	Model railways	Victorian marriage
Feeding babies	Money	Volcanoes
First atomic bomb	Money management	Water
Food	Mountain biking	The Wild West
Forgery	Multiple sclerosis	Wine

Genres		
Advice booklet	History book in style of tabloid newspaper	Radio 1 programme
Advice tape	Illustrated magazine	Radio 4 programme
Audio guide	Information booklet/pack	Radio 5 programme
Audio-visual presentation	Information pack	Radio trailer
Broadsheet newspaper article	Leaflet	Tabloid newspaper article
CD insert	Literary anthology	Talk
CD-ROM	Newspaper supplement	Theatre programme
Commentary for a slide show	Popular encyclopaedia	Wall chart/information board
Dramatised radio documentary	Presentation pack/illustrated fact sheets	Web pages
Educational resource pack		Woman's Hour
Faction		

Audiences		
Adult beginners	General public	Passengers, travellers
Children 7–11	Key Stage 2 pupils	Patients, family, relatives and friends
Children 9–13	Museum, theatre, attraction visitors	School and college leavers
Children 11–15	Parents	Young adults
GCSE students